Heaven Is For Real

Spurgeon Sermons on the Hope of Every Believer

Charles H. Spurgeon

Bibliographical Information

This volume is a collection of sermons delivered by Charles Spurgeon (1834–1892) between 1855 and 1868. His writings were originally published in book form by Passmore & Alabaster in London, England in the late nineteenth century.

an Ichthus Publications edition

Contents

1

Citizenship In Heaven

"For our citizenship is in heaven; from where we also look for the Saviour, the Lord Jesus Christ."

—Philippians 3:20

THERE CAN BE NO COMPARISON between a soaring seraph and a crawling worm. Christian men ought so to live so that it would be idle to speak of a comparison between them and the men of the world. It should not be a comparison but a contrast. No scale of degrees should be possible; the believer should be a direct and obvious contradiction to the unregenerate. The life of a saint should be altogether above, and not in the same category as the life of a sinner. We should compel our critics not to confess that moralists are good, and Christians a little better; but while the world is darkness, we should obviously be light; and while the world lies in the Wicked One, we should most evidently be of God, and overcome the temptations of that Wicked One. Wide as the poles apart, are life and death, light and darkness, health and disease, purity and sin, spiritual and carnal, divine and sensual. If we were what we profess to be, we should be as distinct a people in the midst of this world, as white men in a community of Ethiopians, there should be no more difficulty in detecting the Christian from the worldling than in determining a sheep from a goat, or a lamb from a wolf. Alas! the Church is so much adulterated, that we have to abate our glorying, and cannot exalt her character as we wish. "The precious sons of Zion, comparable to fine gold, how are they esteemed as earthen pitchers, the work of the hands of the potter!" Oh for the time when "our citizenship shall be in heaven," and the ignoble life of the man, whose god is his belly and whose end is destruction, shall be rebuked by our unworldly, unselfish character. There should be as much difference between the worldling and the Christian as between hell and heaven, between destruction and eternal life. As we hope at last that there shall be a great gulf separating us from the doom of the impenitent, there should be here a deep and wide gulf between us and the ungodly. The purity of our character should be such, that men must take knowledge of us that we are of another and superior race. God grant us more and more to be most clearly a chosen generation, a royal priesthood, a holy

5

nation, a peculiar people, so that we may show forth the praises of him who has called us out of darkness into his marvellous light.

Brethren, tonight I exhort you to holiness, not by the precepts of the law; not by the thunderings from Sinai; not by the perils or punishments which might fall upon you if you are unholy; but by the privileges to which you have been admitted. Gracious souls should only be urged by arguments from grace. Whips are for the backs of fools, and not for heirs of heaven. By the honourable citizenship which has been bestowed upon you, I shall beseech you to let your citizenship be in heaven, and I shall urge that most prevailing argument, that the Lord Jesus Christ comes, and therefore we should be as men who watch for our Lord, diligently doing service for him, so that when he comes he may say to us, "Well done, good and faithful servants." I know that the grace which is in you will freely answer to such a plea.

Our text, I think, might be best translated thus — "Our citizenship is in heaven." The French translation renders it, "As for us, our burgesseship is in the heavens." Doddridge paraphrases it, "But we converse as citizens of heaven, considering ourselves as denizens of the New Jerusalem, and only strangers and pilgrims upon earth."

We Are Aliens Here.

I. The first idea which is suggested by the verse under consideration is this: if our citizenship is in heaven, then WE ARE ALIENS HERE; we are strangers and foreigners, pilgrims and sojourners on the earth, as all our fathers were. In the words of Sacred Writ "Here we have no continuing city," but "we desire a better country, that is a heavenly." Let us illustrate our position. A certain young man is sent out by his father to do business on behalf of the family: he is sent to America, and he is just now living in New York. A very fortunate thing it is for him that his citizenship is in England; that, although he lives in America and does business there, yet he is an alien, and does not belong to that afflicted nation; for he retains his citizenship with us on this side of the Atlantic. Yet there is a line of conduct which is due from him to the country which affords him shelter, and he must see to it that he does not fail to render it. Since we are aliens, we must remember to behave ourselves as aliens should, and by no means come short in our duty. We are affected by the position of our temporary country. A person doing business in New York or Boston, although he is a freeman of the city of London, will find himself very much affected by the business of the Dis-United States: when the merchants of his city suffer, he will find himself suffering with them, the fluctuations of their money market will affect his undertakings, and the stagnation of commerce will slacken his progress; but if prosperity should happily return, he will find that when the coffers of their merchants are getting full, his will be the better; and the happy development of trade will give buoyancy to his own ventures. He is not a citizen of the nation, and yet every trembling of the scale will affect him; he will prosper as that nation prospers, and he will suffer as that nation suffers; that is to say, not as a citizen, but as a businessman. And so we in this country find that, although we are strangers and foreigners on earth, yet we share all the inconveniences of the flesh. No exemption is granted to us from the common lot of manhood. We are born to trouble, even as others, and have troubles like the rest. When famine comes we hunger; and when war rages we are in danger; exposed to the same clime, bearing the same burning heat, or the same freezing cold; we know the whole train of ills, even as the citizens of earth know them. When God in mercy scatters liberally with both his hands the bounties of his providence, we take our share, although we are aliens, yet we live upon the good of the land, and share the tender mercies of the God of Providence. Hence we have to take some interest in it; and the good man, although he is a foreigner, will not live even a week in this foreign land without *seeking to do good* among the neighbours with whom he lives. The good Samaritan sought not only the good of the Samaritan nation, but of the Jews. Although there was no tie of kinship among them (for the Samaritans were not, as we have often heard erroneously said, first cousins or relatives to the Jews; not a drop of Jewish blood ever ran in the Samaritans' veins; they were strangers brought from Assyria; they had no relationship to Abraham whatever) yet the good Samaritan, finding himself travelling between Jericho and Jerusalem, did good to the Jew, since he was in Judea. The Lord charged his people by his servant Jeremiah, "Seek the peace of the city to where I have caused you to be carried away captives, and pray to the Lord for it: for in its peace you shall have peace." Since we are here, we must seek the good of this world. "To do good and do not forget to share." "Love your enemies, and do good, and lend, hoping for nothing again; and your reward shall be great, and you shall be the children of the Highest: for he is kind to the unthankful and to the evil." We must do our utmost while we are here to bring men to Christ, to win them from their evil ways, to bring them to eternal life, and to make them, with us, citizens of another and a better land; for, to tell the truth, we are here as recruiting sergeants for heaven; here to give men the enlisting money, to bind upon them the blood red colours of the Saviour's service, to win them to King Jesus, so that, by and by, they may share his victories after having fought his battles.

Seeking the good of the country as aliens, we must also remember that it behooves aliens to *keep themselves very quiet.* What business have foreigners to plot against the government, or to intermeddle with the politics of a country in which they have no citizenship? An Englishman in New York had best be without a tongue just now; if he should criticise the courage of the generals, the accuracy of their despatches, or the genius of the President, he might meet with rather rough usage. He will be injudicious indeed, if he cannot leave America to the Americans. So, in this land of ours, where you and I are strangers, we must be orderly sojourners, submitting ourselves constantly to those who are in authority, leading orderly and peaceable lives, and, according to the command of the Holy Spirit through the apostle, "honouring all men, fearing God, honouring the king"; "submitting ourselves to every ordinance of man for the Lord's sake." I cannot say that I delight in political Christians; I fear that party strife is a serious trial to believers, and I cannot reconcile our heavenly citizenship with the schemes of the hustings and the riot of the polling booth. You must follow your own judgment here, but for my part, I am a foreigner even in England, and as such I mean to act. We are simply passing through this earth, and should bless it in our transit, but never yoke ourselves to its affairs. An Englishman may happen to be in Spain — he wishes a thousand things were different from what they are, but he does not trouble himself much about them: he says, "If I were a Spaniard I would see what I could do to alter this government, but, being an Englishman, let the Spaniards see to their own matters. I shall be back to my own country by and by, and the sooner the better." So with Christians here; they are content very much to let the potsherds strive with the potsherds of the earth; their politics concern their own country, they do not care much about any other; as men they love liberty, and are not willing to lose it even in the lower sense; but, spiritually, their politics are spiritual, and as citizens they look to the interest of that divine republic to which they belong, and they wait for the time when, having patiently borne with the laws of the land of their banishment, they shall come under the more benevolent sway of him who reigns in glory, the King of kings, and Lord of lords. If it is possible, as much as lies in you, live peaceably with all men, and still serve your day and generation, but do not build your soul's dwelling place here, for all this earth must be destroyed at the coming of the fiery day.

Again, let us remember that as aliens *we have privileges as well as duties.* The princes of evil cannot draft us into their regiments; we cannot be compelled to do Satan's work. The king of this world may make his vassals serve him, but he cannot raise a conscription upon aliens. He may order out his troops to this villany, or to that dastardly service, but the child of God claims an immunity from all the commands of Satan; let evil maxims bind the men that own their sway, we are free, and do not own the prince of the power of the air. I know that men of this world say we must keep up appearances; we must be respectable; we must do as others do; we must swim with the tide; we must move with the crowd; but not so the upright believer: "No," he says, "Do not expect me to fall in with your ways and customs; I am in Rome, but I shall not do as Rome does. I will let you see that I am an alien, and that I have rights as an alien, even here in this foreign land. I am not to be bound to fight your battles, nor march to the sound of your drums." Brethren, we are soldiers of Christ; we are enlisted in *his* army; and as aliens here, we are not to be constrained into the army of evil. Let lords and lands have what masters they wish, let us be free, for Christ is still our Master. The seven thousand whom God has reserved, will not bow the knee to Baal. Let it be known to you, oh world, that we will not serve your gods, nor worship the image which you have set up. We are servants of God, and we will not be in bondage to men.

Just as we are free from the conscription of the State, so we must remember, also, that we are not eligible for its honours. I know you will say that is not a privilege; but it is a great boon if looked at properly. An Englishman in New York is not eligible for the very prickly throne of the President; I suppose he could not well be made a governor of Massachusetts or any other State, and, indeed, he may be well content to renounce the difficulties and the honour too. So also, the Christian man here is not eligible for this world's honours. It is a very ill omen to hear the world clap its hands, and say "Well done" to the Christian man. He may begin to look at his standing, and wonder whether he has not been doing wrong when the unrighteous give him their approbation. "What, did I do wrong," said Socrates, "that that villain praised me just now?" And so may the Christian say, "What, have I done wrong, that So-and-so spoke well of me, for if I had done right he would not; he does not have the sense to praise goodness, he could only have applauded what suited his own taste." Christian men, you must never covet the world's esteem; the love of this world is not in keeping with the love of God. "If any man loves the world the love of the Father is not in him." Treat its smiles as you treat its threats, with quiet contempt. Be willing rather to be sneered at than to be approved, counting the cross of Christ greater riches than all the treasures of Egypt. Oh prostitute world, it would be a sad dishonour to be your favourite. Tire your head and paint your face, you Jezebel, but you are no friend of ours, nor will we desire your hollow love. The men of this world would be mad to raise us to their seats of honour, for we are aliens and citizens of another country. When the Pope sent a noted Protestant statesman a present of some silver goblets, he returned them with this answer — "The citizens of Zurich compel their judges to swear twice in the year that they will receive no presents from foreign princes, therefore take them back." More than twice in the year should the Christian resolve that he will not accept the smiles of this world, and will do no homage to its glory. "We fear the Greeks even when they bear gifts." Like the Trojans of old, we may be beguiled with presents even if unconquered in arms. Reject then the grandeur and honour of this fleeting age. Say in life, what a proud cardinal said in death, "Vain pomp and glory of the world, I hate you." Pass through Vanity Fair without trading in its vanities; crying, in answer to their "What will you buy?" — "We buy the truth." Take up the pilgrim's song and always sing it —

> The things eternal I pursue,
> And happiness beyond the view,
>   Of those who basely pant;
> For things by nature felt and seen;
> Their honours, wealth, and pleasures mean,
>   I neither have nor want.
> Nothing on earth I call my own:
> A stranger to the world unknown,
>   I all their goods despise;
> I trample on their whole delight,
> And seek a country out of sight, —
>   A country in the skies.

Furthermore, as aliens, *it is not for us to hoard up this world's treasures.* Gentlemen, you who know the stock exchange of New York, would you hoard up any extensive amount of Mr. Chase's green backed notes? I do not think so. Those stamps which officiate in the States in lieu of copper coinage I should hardly desire to accumulate; perhaps the fire might consume them, or if not, the gradual process of wear and tear which they are sure to undergo might leave me penniless before long. "No, sir," says the British businessman, "I am an alien; I cannot very well accept payment in these bits of paper, they are very well for you; they will pass as currency in your state, but my riches must be riches in England, for I am going there to live directly; I must have solid gold, old English sovereigns, nothing else except these can make me rich." Brethren, so it is with us. If we are aliens, the treasures of this world are like those bits of paper, of little value in our esteem; and we should lay up our treasure in heaven, "where neither moth nor rust corrupts, and where thieves do not break through nor steal." The money of this world is worthless in Paradise; and when we reach its blissful shore, if regret can be known, we shall wish that we had laid up more treasure in the land of our fatherhood, in the dear fatherland beyond the skies. Transport your jewels to a safer country than this world; be rich toward God rather than before men. A certain minister collecting for a chapel, called upon a rich merchant, who generously gave him fifty pounds. As the good man was going out with sparkling eye at the liberality of the merchant, the tradesman opened a letter, and he said, "Stop a minute, I find by this letter, I have lost this morning a ship worth six thousand pounds." The poor minister trembled in his shoes, for he thought the next word would be, "Let me have the fifty pound cheque back." Instead of it, it was "Let me have the cheque back a moment," and then taking out his pen he wrote him a cheque for five hundred pounds. "Since my money is going so fast, it is well," he said, "to make sure of some of it, so I will put some of it in God's bank." The man, you do not doubt, went his way astonished at such a way of dealing as this, but indeed that is just what a man should do, who feels he is an alien here, and his treasure is beyond the sky.

> There is my house and portion fair;
> My treasure and my heart are there,
>   And my abiding home:
> For me my elder brethren stay,
> And angels beckon me away,
>   And Jesus bids me come.

We Are Citizens in Heaven.

II. It is our comfort now to remind you that although aliens *on earth*, WE ARE CITIZENS IN HEAVEN.

What is meant by our being citizens in heaven? Why, first that *we are under heaven's government.* Christ the King of heaven reigns in our hearts; the laws of glory are the laws of our consciences; our daily prayer is, "Your will be done on earth as it is in heaven." The proclamations issued from the throne of glory are freely received by us, the decrees of the Great King we cheerfully obey. We are not without law to Christ. The Spirit of God rules in our mortal bodies, grace reigns through righteousness, and we wear the easy

11

yoke of Jesus. Oh that he would sit as King in our hearts, like Solomon upon his throne of gold. Yours are we, Jesus, and all that we have; rule without a rival.

As citizens of the New Jerusalem, *we share heaven's honours*. The glory which belongs to beatified saints belongs to us, for we are already sons of God, already princes of the imperial blood; already we wear the spotless robe of Jesus' righteousness; already we have angels for our servants, saints for our companions, Christ for our brother, God for our Father, and a crown of immortality for our reward. We share the honours of citizenship, for we have come to the general assembly and Church of the firstborn, whose names are written in heaven. "Beloved, now we are the sons of God, and it does not yet appear what we shall be: but we know that, when he shall appear, we shall be like him; for we shall see him as he is."

As citizens, *we have common rights in all the property of heaven*. Those wide extensive plains we sang about just now are ours; ours those harps of gold and crowns of glory; ours the gates of pearl and walls of chrysolite; ours the azure light of the city that needs no candle nor light of the sun; ours the river of the water of life, and the twelve manner of fruits which grow on the trees planted at its side; there is nothing in heaven that does not belong to us, for our citizenship is there. "Things present, or things to come; all are ours; and we are Christ's; and Christ is God's."

And just as we are thus under heaven's government, and share its honours and partake of its possessions, so we today *enjoy its delights*. Do they rejoice over sinners who are born to God — prodigals who have returned? So do we. Do they chant the glories of triumphant grace? We do the same. Do they cast their crowns at Jesus' feet? Such honours as we have, we cast there too. Do they rejoice in him? So also do we. Do they triumph, waiting for his second advent? By faith we triumph in the same. Are they tonight singing, "Worthy is the Lamb?" We also have sung the same tune, not to such glorious notes as theirs, but with as sincere hearts; with melody not quite so splendid, but we hope as sincere, for the Spirit gave us the music, which we have, and the Spirit gave them the thunders of their acclamations before the throne. "Our citizenship is in heaven."

Brethren, we rejoice to know also that as the result of our being citizens, or rather I ought to have said as the cause of it, our *names are written in the roll* of heaven's freemen. When, at last, the list shall be read, our names shall be read too; for where Paul and Peter, where David and Jonathan, where Abraham and Jacob shall be found, we shall be found too; numbered with them we were in the divine purpose, reckoned with them we were in the purchase on the cross, and with them we shall sit down for ever at the tables of the blessed. The small and the great are fellow citizens and of the same household. The babes and the perfect men are recorded in the same great registry, and neither death nor hell can erase a single name.

Our citizenship then is in heaven. We do not have time to expand that thought. John Calvin says of this text, "It is a most abundant source of many exhortations, which it would be easy for any one to elicit from it." We are not all Calvins; but even to our smaller capacities, the subject appears to be one not readily exhausted, but rich with unfathomable joy.

Our Citizenship Is in Heaven.

III. We must now come to our third point, which is, OUR CITIZENSHIP IS IN HEAVEN, our walk and acts are such as are consistent with our dignity *as citizens of heaven.* Among the old Romans, when a dastardly action was proposed, it was thought a sufficient refusal to answer *"Romanus sum* — I am a Roman." Surely it should be a strong incentive for every good thing if we can claim to be freemen of the Eternal City. Let our lives be conformed to the glory of our citizenship. In heaven they are holy, so must we be — so are we if our citizenship is not a mere pretence. They are happy, so must we be rejoicing in the Lord always. In heaven they are obedient, so must we be, following the faintest directives of the divine will. In heaven they are active, so should we be, both day and night praising and serving God. In heaven they are peaceful, so should we find a rest in Christ and be at peace even now. In heaven they rejoice to behold the face of Christ, so we should be always meditating upon him, studying his beauties, and desiring to look into the truths which he has taught. In heaven they are full of love, so we should love one another as brethren. In heaven they have sweet communion with each other, so we should, who though many, are one body, each being members of each other. Before the throne they are free from envy and strife, ill will, jealousy, emulation, falsehood, anger, so should we be: we should, in fact, try while we are here to keep up the manners and customs of the good old fatherland, so that, as in Paris, the Parisian soon says, "There goes John Bull," so they should be able to say in this land, "there goes a heavenly citizen, one who is with us, and among us, but is not of us." Our very speech should be such that our citizenship should be detected. We should not be able to live long in a house without men finding out what we are. A friend of mine once went across to America, and landing I think at Boston, he knew no one, but hearing a man say, when someone had dropped a cask on the wharf, "Look out there, or else you will make a Coggeshall job of it." He said, "You are an Essex man I know, for that is a proverb never used anywhere except in Essex: give me your hand"; and they were friends at once. So there should be a ring of true metal about our speech and conduct, so that when a brother meets us, he can say "You are a Christian, I know, for no one except Christians speak like that, or act like that." "You also were with Jesus of Nazareth, for your speech betrays you." Our holiness should act as a sort of freemasonry by which we know how to give the grip to the stranger, who is not a real stranger, but a fellow citizen with us, and of the household of faith. Oh! dear friends, wherever we wander, we should never forget our beloved land. In Australia, on the other side the world, or in the Cape of Good Hope, or wherever else we may be exiled, surely every Englishman's eye must turn to this fair island; and with all her faults, we must love her still. And surely let us be where we may, our eyes must turn to heaven, the happy land unstained by shadow of fault; we love her still, and love her more and more, praying for the time when our banishment shall expire, and we shall enter into our fatherland to dwell there for ever and ever. Shenstone says, "The proper means of increasing the love we bear for our native country, is to reside some time in a foreign land." I am sure that we who cry, "Woe is me, for I dwell in Mesech, and sojourn in the tents of Kedar!" are sure to add "Oh that I had wings like a dove, for then I would fly away, and be at rest."

Our Commerce Is in Heaven.

IV. The text says, "Our citizenship is in heaven," and I think we may read it, as though it said, "OUR COMMERCE IS IN HEAVEN." We are doing business on earth, but still the bulk of our business is with heaven. We trade for trinkets in this land, but our gold and silver are in heaven.

We commune with heaven, and how? Our business is with heaven by *meditation,* we often think of God our Father, and Christ our Brother; and, by the Spirit, the Comforter, we are brought in contemplative delight, to the general assembly and Church of the firstborn, whose names are written in heaven. Brethren, do not our *thoughts* sometimes burn within us, when we do business with that blessed land. When I have sent the ships of understanding and consideration to that land of Ophir, which is full of gold, and they have come back again laden with all manner of precious things, my thoughts have been enriched, my soul has longed to journey to that good land. Black and stormy are you, oh sea of death, but I wish to cross you to reach that land of Havilah, which has dust of gold. I know that he who is a Christian will never have his mind off that better land for very long. And do you know we sometimes do business with heaven in our *hymns.* They tell us about the Swiss soldiery in foreign countries, that there is a song which the band is forbidden to play, because it reminds them of the cowbells of their native hills. If the men hear it, they are sure to desert, for that dear old song revives before their eyes the wooden chalets and the cows, and the pastures of the glorious Alps, and they long to be away. There are some of our hymns that make us homesick, until we are hardly content to stop, and therefore, well did our poet end his song,

> Filled with delight, my raptured soul,
>> Can here no longer stay.
> Though Jordan's waves around us roll,
>> Fearless we launch away.
> I feel the spirit of Wesley, when he said —
> Oh that we now might see our guide!
>> Oh that the word were given!
> Come, Lord of hosts, the waves divide,
>> And land us all in heaven.

In times of high, hallowed, heavenly harmony of praise, the songs of angels seem to come astray, and find their way down to us, and then our songs return with them, hand in hand, and go back to God's throne, through Jesus Christ.

We do business with heaven, I hope, too, not only thus by meditation, and by thought, and by song, but *by hopes and by loves*. Our love is toward that land. How heartily the Germans sing of the dear old fatherland; but they cannot, with all their Germanic patriotism, they cannot beat the genial glow of the Briton's heart, when he thinks of his fatherland too. The Scotchman, too, wherever he may be, remembers the land of "brown heath and shaggy wood." And the Irishman, too, wherever he is, still thinks the "Emerald Isle" to be the first gem of the sea. It is right that the patriot should love his country. Does not our love fervently flame towards heaven? We think we cannot speak well enough of it, and indeed here we are correct, for no exaggeration is possible. When we talk about that land of Eshcol, our mouths are watering to taste its clusters; already, like David, we thirst to drink from the well that is within the gate; and we hunger after the good grain of the land. Our ears are wanting to be done with the discords of earth, so that they may open to the harmonies of heaven; and our tongues are longing to sing the melodious sonnets, sung by flaming ones above. Yes, we do love heaven, and thus it is that we prove that our commerce is with that better land.

Brethren, just as people in a foreign land who love their country always are glad to have plenty of letters from the country, I hope we have much *communication with the old fatherland.* We send our prayers there as letters to our Father, and we get his letters back in this blessed volume of his Word. You go into an Australian settler's hut, and you find a newspaper. Where is it from, sir? A gazette from the south of France, a journal from America? Oh no, it is a newspaper from England, addressed to him in his old mother's handwriting, bearing the postage stamp with the good Queen's face in the corner; and he likes it, although it is only a newspaper from some little pottering country town, with no news in it; yet he likes it better, perhaps, than the "Times" itself, because it tells him about the village where he lived, and consequently touches a special string in the harp of his soul. So must it be with heaven. This book, the Bible, is the newspaper of heaven, and therefore we must love it. The sermons which are preached are good news from a far country. The hymns we sing are notes by which we tell our Father of our welfare here, and by which he whispers into our soul his continued love for us. All these are and must be pleasant to us, for our commerce is with heaven. I hope, too, we are sending a good deal home. I like to see our young fellows when they go out to live in the bush, remember their mother at home. They say, "She had a hard struggle to bring us up when our father died, and she scraped her little together to help us to emigrate." John and Tom mutually agree, "the first gold we get at the diggings we will send home to mother." And it goes home. Well, I hope you are sending a great many things home. Dear friends, I hope since we are aliens here, we are not laying up our treasure here, where we may lose it, but packing it off as quickly as we can to our own country. There are many ways of doing it. God has many banks; and they are all safe ones. We have only to serve his Church, or serve the souls which Christ has bought with his blood, or help his poor, clothe his naked, and feed his hungry, and we send our treasures beyond the sea in a safe ship, and so we keep up our commerce with the skies.

Christ Is Coming Soon.

V. Time has gone; those clocks will strike when they should not. There is a great reason why we should live like aliens and foreigners here, and that is, CHRIST IS COMING SOON. The early Church never forgot this. Did they not pant and thirst after the return of their ascended Lord? Like the twelve tribes, day and night they instantly watched for the Messiah. But the Church has grown weary of this hope. There have been so many false prophets who tell us that Christ is coming, that the Church thinks he never will come; and she begins to deny, or to keep in the background the blessed

16

doctrine of the second advent of her Lord from heaven. I do not think the fact that there have been many false prophets should make us doubt our Lord's true word. Perhaps the very frequency of these mistakes may show that there is truth at the bottom. You have a friend who is ill, and the doctor says he cannot last long; he must die; you have called a great many times expecting to hear of his departure, but he is still alive; now the frequent errors of the physicians do not prove that your friend will not die one of these days, and that speedily too. And so, although the false prophets have said, "Lo, here," and "Lo, there," and yet Christ has not come, that does not prove that his glorious appearing will never arrive. You know I am no prophet. I do not know anything about the next decade; I find quite enough to do to attend to this year. I do not understand the visions of Daniel or Ezekiel; I find I have enough to do to teach the simple word such as I find in Matthew, Mark, Luke, and John, and the Epistles of Paul. I do not find many souls have been converted to God by exquisite dissertations about the battle of Armageddon, and all those other fine things; I have no doubt prophesyings are very profitable, but I rather question whether they are so profitable to the hearers, as they may be to the preachers and publishers. I conceive that among religious people of a certain kind, the abortive explanations of prophecy issued by certain doctors gratify a craving which in irreligious people finds its food in novels and romances. People have a panting to know the future; and certain divines pander to this depraved taste, by prophesying for them, and letting them know what is coming by and by. I do not know the future, and I shall not pretend to know. But I do preach this, because I know it, that *Christ will come*, for he says so in a hundred passages. The Epistles of Paul are full of the advent, and Peter's too, and John's letters are crowded with it. The best of saints have always lived on the hope of the advent. There was Enoch, he prophesied of the coming of the Son of Man. So there was another Enoch who was always talking about the coming, and saying, "Come quickly." I will not divide the house tonight by discussing whether the advent will be premillennial or post millennial, or anything of that, it is enough for me that *he will come*, and "in such an hour as you do not think, the Son of Man will come." Tonight he may appear, while we stand here; just when we think that he will not come, the thief shall break into the house. We ought, therefore, to be always watching. Since the gold and silver that you have will be worthless at his advent; since your lands and estates will melt into smoke when he appears; since, *then* the righteous shall be rich, and the godly shall be great, do not lay up your treasure here, for it may at any time vanish, at any time disappear, for Christ may come at any moment.

17

I think the Church would do well to be always living as if Christ might come today. I feel persuaded she is doing poorly if she works as if he would not come until the next decade, because he may come before, and he may come this moment. Let her always be living as if he would come *now*, still acting in her Master's sight, and watching to prayer. Never mind about the last vials, fill your own vial with sweet odours and offer it before the Lord. Think what you like about Armageddon; but do not forget to fight the good fight of faith. Do not guess at the precise era for the destruction of Antichrist, go and destroy it yourself, fighting against it every day; but be looking forward and hastening to the coming of the Son of Man; and let this be at once your comfort and incentive for diligence — that the Saviour will soon come from heaven.

Now, I think you foreigners here present — and I hope there are a great many true aliens here — ought to feel like a poor stranded mariner on a desolate island, who has saved a few things from the wreck and built himself an old log hut, and has a few comforts all around him, but for all that he longs for home. Every morning he looks out to sea, and wonders when he shall see a sail; many times while examining the wide ocean to look for a ship, he has clapped his hands, and then wept to find he was disappointed; every night he lights his fire so that there may be a blaze, so that if a ship should go by, they may send relief to the stranded mariner. Ah! that is just the way we ought to live. We have heard of one saint who used to open his window every morning when he woke up, to see if Christ had come; it might be fanaticism, but better to be enthusiastic than to mind earthly things. I would have us look out each night and light the fire of prayer, so that it may be burning in case the ships of heaven should go by, so that blessings may come to us poor aliens and foreigners who need them so much. Let us wait patiently until the Lord's convoy shall take us on board, so that we may be carried into the glories and splendour of the reign of Christ, let us always hold the log hut with a loose hand, and long for the time when we shall get to that better land where our possessions are, where our Father lives, where our treasures lie, where all our brethren dwell. Well said our poet —

> Blest scenes, through rude and stormy seas
> I onward press to you.

My beloved friends, I can assure you it is always one of the sweetest thoughts I have ever known, that I shall meet with you in heaven. There are so many of you members of this Church, that I can hardly get to shake hands with you once in a year; but I shall have plenty of time then in heaven. You will know your pastor in heaven better than you do now. He loves you now, and you love him. We shall then have more time to recount our experience of divine grace, and praise God together, and sing together, and rejoice together concerning him by whom we were helped to plant, and sow, and through whom all the increase came.

> I hope when days and years are past,
> We all shall meet in heaven,
> We all shall meet in heaven at last,
> We all shall meet in heaven.

But we shall not all meet in glory; not all, unless you repent. Some of you will certainly perish, unless you believe in Christ. But why must we be divided? Oh! why are we not all in heaven? "Believe in the Lord Jesus Christ, and you shall be saved." "He who believes and is baptized shall be saved, but he who does not believe shall be damned." Trust Christ, sinner, and heaven is yours, and mine, and we are safe for ever. Amen.

2

The Heavenly Race

"So run, that ye may obtain."

—1 Corinthians 9:24

WE ARE CONTINUALLY INSISTING UPON it from day to day, that salvation is not of works, but of grace. We lay this down as one of the very first doctrines of the gospel. "Not of works, lest any man should boast." "By grace are ye saved, through faith, and that not of yourselves; it is the gift of God." But we find that it is equally necessary to preach the absolute necessity of a religious life for the attainment of heaven at last. Although we are sure that men are not saved for the sake of their works, yet are we equally sure that no man will be saved without them; and that he who leads an unholy life, who neglects the great salvation, can never inherit that crown of life which fadeth not away. In one sense, true religion is wholly the work of God; yet there are high and important senses in which we must ourselves "strive to enter in at the strait gate." We must run a race; we must wrestle even to agony; we must fight a battle, before we can inherit the crown of life. We have in our text the course of religion set down as a race; and inasmuch as there be many who enter upon a profession of religion with very false motives, the apostle warns us that although all run in a race, yet all do not obtain the prize: they run all, but only one is rewarded: and he gives us, therefore, the practical exhortation to run that we may obtain; for unless we are the winners we had better not have been runners at all; for he that is not a winner is a loser; he who makes a profession of religion, and does not at last obtain the crown of life, is a loser by his profession; for his profession was hypocrisy or else formality, and he had better not have made a profession, than fall therein.

And now, in entering upon the text, I shall have to notice *what it is we are to run for:* "So run that ye may *obtain;"* secondly, *the mode o*f running, to which we must attend—"So run that ye may obtain;" and then I shall give a few *practical exhortations* to stir those onward in the heavenly race who are flagging and negligent, in order that they may at last "obtain."

I. In the first place, then, WHAT IS IT THAT WE OUGHT TO SEEK TO OBTAIN?

Some people think they must be religious, *in order to be respectable.* There are a vast number of people in the world who go to church and to chapel, because everybody else does so. It is disreputable to waste your Sundays, not to be found going up to the house of God, therefore they take a pew and attend the services, and they think they have done their duty: they have obtained all that they sought for, when they can hear their neighbors saying, "Such-and-such a man is a very respectable person; he is always very regular at his Church; he is a very reputable person, and exceedingly praiseworthy." Verily, if this be what you seek after in your religion, you shall get it; for the Pharisees who sought the praise of men "had their reward." But when you have gotten it, what a poor reward it is! Is it worth the drudgery? I do not believe that the drudgery to which people submit in order to be called respectable, is at an compensated by what they gain. I am sure, for my own part, I would not care a solitary rap what I was called, or what I was thought; nor would I perform anything that was irksome to myself for the sake of pleasing any man that ever walked beneath the stars, however great or mighty he may be. It is the sign of a fawning, cringing spirit, when people are always seeking to do that which renders them respectable. The esteem of men is not worth the looking after, and sad it is, that this should be the only prize which some men put before them, in the poor religion which they undertake.

There are people who go a little farther: they are not content with being considered respectable, but they want something more; *they desire to be considered pre-eminently saints.* These persons come to our places of worship, and after a little time they venture to come forward and ask whether they may unite with our churches. We examine them, and so hidden is their hypocrisy that we cannot discover its rottenness: we receive them into our churches; they sit at the Lord's Supper; they come to our church-meetings: mayhap, they are even voted into the deacon's office; sometimes they attain to the pulpit, though God has never called them, and preach what they have never felt in their hearts. Men may do all this merely to enjoy the praise of men; and they will even undergo some persecution for the sake of it; because to be thought a saint, to be reckoned by religious people to be everything that is right and proper, to have a name among the living in Zion, is to some persons a thing exceedingly coveted. They would not like to be set down among the "chief of sinners," but if they may have their names written among the chief of saints they will consider themselves exceedingly exalted. I am afraid we have a considerable admixture of persons of this sort in our churches who only come for the mere sake of keeping up their religious pretensions and obtaining a religious status in the midst of the church of God. "Verily, I say unto you *they have* their reward," and they shall never have any but what they obtain here. They get their reward for a little time. For a short time they are looked up to. But perhaps even in this life they make a trip, and down they go; the church discovers them, and they are sent out like the ass stripped of the lion's skin to browse once more among their native nettles, no longer to be glorious in the midst of the church of the living God. Or mayhap, they may wear the cloak until the last day of their lives, and then death comes, and strips them of all their tinsel and gewgaw; And they who acted upon the stage of religion as kings and princes, are sent behind the stage to be unrobed and to find themselves beggars to their shame, and naked to their eternal disgrace. It is not this which you and I would seek after in religion. Dearly beloved, if we do run the race, we would run for a higher and more glorious prize than any of these things.

Another set of people take up with religious life for *what they can get by it*. I have known tradespeople attend church for the mere sake of getting the custom of those who went there. I have heard of such things as people knowing which side their bread was buttered, and going to that particular denomination, where they thought they could get the most by it. Loaves and fishes drew some of Christ's followers, and they are very attracting baits, even to this day. Men find there is something to be gotten by religion. Among the poor it is, perhaps, some little charity to be obtained, and among those that are in business, it is the custom which they think to get. "Verily I say unto you, they have their reward;" for the church is ever foolish and unsuspicious. We do not like to suspect our fellow creatures of following us from sordid motives. The church does not like to think that a man would be base enough to pretend to religion for the mere sake of what he can get, and, therefore, we let these people easily slip through, and they have their reward. But ah! at what a price they buy it! They have deceived the Lord's servants for gold, and they have entered into his church as base hypocrites for the sake of a piece of bread; and they shall be thrust out at last with the anger of God behind them, like Adam driven out of Eden, with the flaming Cherubim with a sword turning every way to keep the tree of life; and they shall for ever look back upon this as the most fearful crime they have committed—that they pretended to be God's people when they were not, and entered into the midst of the fold when they were but wolves in sheeps' clothing.

There is yet another class, and when I have referred to them I will mention no more. These are the people who take up with religion for the sake of *quieting their conscience,* and it is astonishing how little of religion will sometimes do that. Some people tell us that if in the time of storm men would pour bottles of oil upon the waves, there would be a great calm at once. I have never tried it, and it is most probable I never shall, for my organ of credulity is not large enough to accept so extensive a statement. But there are some people who think that they can calm the storm of a troubled conscience by pouring a little of the oil of a profession about religion upon it; and it is amazing how wonderful an effect this really has. I have known a man who was drunk many times in a week, and who got his money dishonestly, and yet he always had an easy conscience by going to his church or chapel regularly on the Sunday. We have heard of a man who could "devour widows' houses"—a lawyer who could swallow up everything that came in his way, and yet he would never go to bed without saying his prayers; and that stilled his conscience. We have heard of other persons, especially among the Romanists, who would not object to thieving, but who would regard eating anything but fish on a Friday as a most fearful sin, supposing that by making a fast on the Friday, all the iniquities of all the days in the week would be put away. They want the outward forms of religion to keep the conscience quiet; for Conscience is one of the worst lodgers to have in your house when he gets quarrelsome: there is no abiding with him; he is an ill bed-fellow; ill at lying down, and equally troublesome at rising up. A guilty conscience is one of the curses of the world: it puts out the sun, and takes away the brightness from the moonbeam. A guilty conscience casts a noxious exhalation through the air, removes the beauty from the landscape, the glory from the flowing river, the majesty from the rolling floods. There is nothing beautiful to the man that has a guilty conscience. He needs no accusing; everything accuses him. Hence people take up with religion just to quiet them. They take the sacrament sometimes; they go to a place of worship; they sing a hymn now and then, they give a guinea to a charity; they intend to leave a portion in their will to build alms-houses, and in this way conscience is lulled asleep, and they rock him to and fro with religious observances, till there he sleeps while they sing over him the lullaby of hypocrisy, and he wakes not until he shall wake with that rich man who was here clothed in purple, but in the next world did lift up his eyes in hell, being in torments, without a drop of water to cool his burning tongue.

What, then, is it, for which we ought to run in this race? Why heaven, eternal life, justification by faith, the pardon of sin, acceptance in the Beloved, and glory everlasting. If you run for anything else than salvation, should you will, what you have won is not worth the running for. Oh! I beseech every one of you, make sure work for eternity, never be contented with anything less than a living faith in a living Saviour; rest not until you are certain that the Holy Spirit is at work in your souls. Do not think that the outside of religion can be of use to you; it is just the inward part of religion that God loveth. Seek to have a repentance that needeth not to be repented of—a faith which looks alone to Christ, and which will stand by you when you come into the swellings of Jordan, Seek to have a love which is not like a transient flame, burning for a moment and then extinguished; but a flame which shall increase and increase, and still increase, till your heart shall be swallowed up therein, and Jesus Christ's one name shall be the sole object of your affection. We must, in running the heavenly race, set nothing less before us than that which Christ did set before him. He set the joy of salvation before himself, and then he did run, despising the cross and enduring the shame. So let us do; and may God give us good success, that by his good Spirit we may attain unto eternal life, through the resurrection of Jesus Christ our Lord!

II. Thus have I noticed what it is we are to run for. And now the Apostle says, "So run that ye may obtain." I shall notice some people who never will obtain, and tell you the reason why, and in so doing, I shall be illustrating THE RULES OF THE RACE.

There are some people who certainly never will obtain the prize, because they are not even *entered*. Their names are not down for the race, and therefore it is quite clear that they will not run, or if they do run, they will run without having any warrant whatever for expecting to receive the prize. There are some such here this afternoon: who will tell you themselves, "We make no profession, sir—none whatever." It is quite as well, perhaps, that you do not; because if you did, you would be hypocrites, and it is better to make no profession at all than to be hypocrites. Still, recollect, your names are not down for the race, and therefore you cannot win. If a man tells you in business that he makes no profession of being honest, you know that he is a confirmed rogue. If a man makes no profession of being religious, you know what he is—he is irreligious—he has no fear of God before his eyes, he has no love to Christ, he has no hope of heaven. He confesses it himself. Strange that men should be so ready to confess this. You don't find persons in the street willing to acknowledge that they are confirmed drunkards. Generally a man will repudiate it with scorn. You never find a man saying to you, "I don't profess to be a chaste living man." You don't hear another say, "I don't profess to be anything but a covetous wretch." No; people are not so fast about telling their faults: and yet you hear people confess the greatest fault to which man can be addicted: they say, "I make no profession"—which means just this—that they do not give God his due. God has made them, and yet they won't serve him; Christ hath come into the world to save sinners, and yet they will not regard him; the gospel is preached; and yet they will not hear it, they have the Bible in their houses, and yet they will not attend to its admonitions: they make no profession of doing so. It will be short work with them at the last great day. There will be no need for the books to be opened, no need for a long deliberation in the verdict. They do not profess to be pardoned; their guilt is written upon their own foreheads, their brazen shamelessness shall be seen by the whole world, as a sentence of destruction written upon their very brows. You cannot expect to win heaven unless your names are entered for the race. If there be no attempts whatever made, even at so much as a profession of religion, then of course you may just sit down and say, "Heaven is not for me; I have no part nor lot in the inheritance of Israel, I cannot say that my Redeemer liveth; and I may rest quite assured that Tophet is prepared of old *for me*. I must feel its pains and know its miseries; for there are but two places to dwell in hereafter, and if I am not found on the right hand of the Judge, there is but one alternative—namely, to be cast away for ever into the blackness of darkness."

Then there is another class whose names are down, but they *never started right*. A bad start is a sad thing. If in the ancient races of Greece or Rome a man who was about to run for the race had loitered, or if he had started before the time it would not matter how fast he ran, if he did not start in order. The flag must drop before the horse starts; otherwise, even if it reach the winning post first, it shall have no reward. There is something to be noted, then, in the starting of the race. I have known men run the race of religion with all their might, and yet they have lost it because they did not start right. You say, "Well, how is that?" Why, there are some people who on a sudden leap into religion. They get it quickly, and they keep it for a time. and at last they lose it because they did not get their religion the right way. They have heard that before a man can be saved, it is necessary that, by the teaching of the Holy Spirit, he should feel the weight of sin, that he should make a confession of it, that he should renounce all hope in his own works, and should look to Jesus Christ alone. They look upon all these things as unpleasant preliminaries and therefore, before they have attended to repentance, before the Holy Spirit has wrought a good work in them before they have been brought to give up everything and trust to Christ, they make a profession of religion. This is just setting up in business without a stock in trade, and there must be a failure. If a man has no capital to begin with, he may make a fine show for a little time, but it shall be as the crackling of thorns under a pot, a great deal of noise and much light for a little time, but it shall die out in darkness. How many there are who never think it necessary that there should be heart work within! Let us remember, however, that there

25

never was a true new birth without much spiritual suffering, that there never was a man who had a changed heart without his first having a miserable heart. We must pass through that black tunnel of conviction before we can come out upon the high embankment of holy joy; we must first go through the Slough of Despond before we can run along the walls of Salvation. There must be ploughing before there is sowing; there must be many a frost, and many a sharp shower before there is any reaping. But we often act like little children who pluck flowers from the shrubs and plant them in their gardens without roots; then they say how fair and how pretty their little garden is; but wait a little while, and their flowers are withered, because they have no roots. This is an the effect of not having a right start, not having the "root of the matter." What is the good of outward religion, the flower and the leaf of it, unless we have the "root of the matter" in us—unless we have been digged into by that sharp iron spade of conviction, and have been ploughed with the plough of the Spirit, and then have been sown with the sacred seed of the gospel, in the hope of bringing forth an abundant harvest? There must be a good start; look well to that, for there is no hope of running unless the start be right.

Again, there are some runners in the heavenly race who cannot win because they *carry too much weight.* A light weight, of course, has the advantage. There are come people who have an immensely heavy weight to carry. "How hardly shall a rich man enter into the kingdom of heaven!" What is the reason? Because he carries so much weight; he has so much of the cares and pleasures of this world; he has such a burden that he is not likely to win, unless God should please to give him a mighty mass of strength to enable him to bear it. We find many men willing to be saved, as they say; they receive the word with great joy, but by-and-bye thorns spring up and choke the word. They have so much business to do; they say they must live; they forget they must die. They have such a deal to attend to, they cannot think of living near to Christ. They find they have little time for devotions; morning prayer must be cut short, because their business begins early; they can have no prayer at night, because business keeps them so late. How can they be expected to think of the things of God? They have so much to do to answer this question—"What shall I eat? what shall I drink? and wherewithal shall I be clothed?" It is true they read in the Bible that their Father who is in heaven will take care of them in these things if they will trust him. But they say, "Not so." Those are enthusiasts according to their notions who rely upon providence. They say, the best providence in all the world is hard work; and they say rightly, but they forget that into the bargain of their hard work "it is in vain to rise up early and sit up late, and eat the bread of carefulness; for except the Lord build the house, they labor in vain that build it." You see two men running a race. One of them, as he starts, lays aside every weight, he takes off his garment and away he runs. There goes the other poor fellow, he has a whole load of gold and silver upon his back. Then around his loins he has many distrustful doubts about what shall become of him in the future, what will be his prospects when he grows old, and a hundred other things. He does not know how to roll his burden upon the Lord. See how he flags, poor fellow, and how the other distances him, leaves him far behind, has gained the corner, and is coming to the winning post. It is well for us if we can cast everything away except that one thing needful, and say, "This is my business, to serve God on earth, knowing that I shall enjoy him in heaven." For when we leave our business to God, we leave it in better hands than if we took care of it ourselves. They who carve for themselves generally cut their fingers; but they who leave God to carve for them, shall never have an empty plate. He who will walk after the cloud shall go aright, but he who will run before it shall soon find that he has gone a fool's errand. "Blessed is the man who trusteth in the Lord, and whose hope the Lord.is." "The young lions do lack and suffer hunger, but they that wait upon the Lord shall not want any good thing." Our Saviour said, "Consider the lilies of the field, how they grow; they toil not, neither do they spin, and yet I say unto you that even Solomon in all his glory was not arrayed like one of these." Behold the fowls of the air, for they sow not, neither do they reap, nor gather into barns, yet your heavenly Father feedeth them, are ye not much better than they?" "Trust in the Lord and do good, and verily thou shalt be fed." "His place of defense shall be the munitions of rocks; bread shall be given him; his waters shall be sure." "Seek ye first the kingdom of God and his righteousness, and all these things shall be added unto you." Carry the weight of this world's cares about you. And it will be as much as you can do to carry them and to stand upright under them, but as to running a race with such burdens, it is just impossible.

There is also another thing that will prevent man's running the race. We have known people who stopped on their way to *kick their fellows*. Such things sometimes occur in a race. The horse, instead of speeding onwards to the mark, is of an angry disposition, and sets about kicking those that are running beside him—there is not much probability of his coming in first. "Now they that run in a race run all, but one receiveth the prize." There is one however who never gets it, and that is the man who always attends to his fellow-creatures instead of himself. It is a mysterious thing that I never yet saw a man with a hoe on his shoulder, going to hoe his neighbour's garden, it is a rarity to see a farmer sending his team of horses to plough his neighbour's land; but it is a most singular thing that every day in the week I meet with persons who are attending to other people's character. If they go to the house of God and hear a trite thing said, they say at once "How suitable that was for Mrs. Smith and Mrs. Brown?" The thought never enters their head, how suitable it was to themselves. They lend their ears to everybody else, but they do not hear for themselves. When they get out of chapel, perhaps as they walk home, their first thought is, "Well, how can I find fault with my neighbors?" They think that putting other people down is going up themselves (there never was a greater mistake); that by picking holes in their neighbour's coat they mend their own They have so few virtues of their own that they do not like anybody else to have any therefore they do the best they can to despoil everything good in their neighbor; and it there be a little fault, they will look at it through a magnifying glass, but they will turn the glass the other way when they look at their own sins. Their own faults become exceedingly small while those of others become magnificently great. Now this is a fault not only among professing religious men, but among those who are not religious. We are all so prone to find fault with other people instead of attending to our own home affairs. We attend to the vineyards of others, but our own vineyard we have not kept. Ask a worldly man why he is not religious, and he tells you "Because so-and-so makes a profession of religion and is not consistent." Pray is that any business of yours? To your own Master you must stand or fall, and so must he; God is their judge, and not you. Suppose there are a great many inconsistent Christians—and we are compelled to acknowledge that there are—so much the more reason why you should be a good one. Suppose there are a great many who deceive others; so much the more reason you should set the world an example of what a genuine Christian is. "Ah! but," you say, "I am afraid there are very few." Then why don't you make one? But after all, is that your business? Must not every man bear his own burden? You will not be judged for other men's sins, you will not be saved by their faith, you will not be condemned for their unbelief. Every man must stand in his own proper flesh and blood at the bar of God, to account for the works done in his own body, whether they have been good or whether they have been evil. It will be of little avail for you to say at the day of judgment, "O Lord, I wee looking at my neighbors; O Lord, I was finding fault with the people in the village; I was correcting their follies." But thus saith the Lord: "Did I ever commission thee to be a judge or a divider over them? Why, if thou hadst so much time to spare, and so much critical judgment, didst thou not exercise it upon thyself? Why didst thou not examine thyself, so that thou mightest have been found ready and acceptable in the day of God?" These persons are not very likely to win the race, because they turn to kicking others.

Again, there is another class of persons who will not win the race—namely, those who, although they seem to start very fair, very soon *loiter*. They dart ahead at the first starting, and distance all the others. There they fly away as if they had wings to their heels; but a little further on in the race, it is with difficulty that with whip and spur they are to be kept going at all, and they almost come to a stand still. Alas! this race of persons are to be discovered in all our churches. We get young people who come forward and make a profession of religion, and we talk with them, and we think it is all well with them, and for a little while they do run well; there is nothing wanting in them; we could hold them up as patterns for the imitation of others. Wait a couple of years. They drop off just by little and little. First, perhaps, there is the attendance on a week-day service neglected; then it is altogether discontinued; then one service on Sabbath; then perhaps family prayer, then private prayer—one thing after another is given up, until at last the whole edifice which stood upright and looked so fair, having been built upon the sand, gives way before the shock of time, and down it falls, and great is the ruin thereof. Recollect, it is not starting that wins the race; it is running all the way. He that would be saved, must hold on to the end: "He that endureth to the end, the same shall be saved." Stop and loiter in the race before you have come to the end thereof, and you have made one of the greatest mistakes that could possibly occur. On, on, on! while you live; still onward, onward, onward! for until you come to the grave, you have not come to your resting place until you arrive at the tomb, you have not come to the spot where you may cry "Halt!" Ever onward if ye would win. If you are content to lose, if you would lose your own soul, you may say, "Stop," if you please; but if you would be saved evermore, be on, on, till you have gained the prize.

But there is another class of persons, who are worse than these. They start well too, and they run very fast at first, but at last they leap over the posts and rails, they *go quite out of the course* altogether, and you do not know where they are gone. Every now and then, we get such people as this. They go out from us, because they are not of us, for had they been of us, doubtless they would have continued with us. I might point out in my congregation on the Sabbath-day, a man whom I saw start myself. I saw him running so well I almost envied him the joy he seemed always able to preserve, the faith which ever seemed to be so buoyant and full of jubilee. Alas! just when we thought he was speeding onwards to the prize, some temptation crossed his path, and he turned aside. Away he is scrambling far over the heath, out of the path of right, and men say, "Aha! aha! so would we have it; so would we have it." And they laugh and make merriment over him, because, having once named the name of Jesus Christ, he hath afterwards gone back again, and his last end is worse than the first. Those whom God starts never do this, for they are preserved in Christ Jesus. Those who have been "entered" in the great roll of the Covenant before all eternity shall persevere, by the aid of the good Spirit. He that began the good work in them, shall carry it on even unto the end. But, alas! there are many who run on their own account and in their own strength; and they are like the snail, which as it creeps, leaves its life as a trail upon its own path. They melt away; their nature decayeth; they perish, and where are they? Not in the church, but lost to all hope. They are like the dog that returned to his vomit, and the sow that was washed to her wallowing in the mire. "The last end of that man shall be worse than the first."

I do not think I shall now mention any other class of persons. I have brought before you the rules of the race, if you would will; if you would "so run that you may obtain," you must first of all take care to start well; you must keep to the course; you must keep strait on; you must not stop on the road, or turn aside from it, but, urged on by Divine grace, you must ever fly onwards, "like an arrow from the bow, shot by an archer strong." And never rest until the march is ended, and you are made pillars in the house of your God, to go out no more for ever.

III. But now I am about to give you some few reasons to URGE YOU ONWARD IN THE HEAVENLY RACE—those of you who are already running.

One of my reasons shall be this—*"We are compassed about by so great a cloud of witnesses."* When zealous racers on yonder heath are flying across the plain, seeking to obtain the reward, the whole heath is covered with multitudes of persons, who are eagerly gazing upon them, and no doubt the noise of those who cheer them onward, and the thousand eyes of those who look upon them, have a tendency to make them stretch every nerve, and press with vigor on. It was so in the games to which the apostle alludes. There the people sat on raised platforms, while the racers ran before them, and they cried to them, and the friends of the racers urged them forward, and the kindly voice would ever be heard bidding them go on. Now, Christian brethren, how many witnesses are looking down upon you. Down! do I say? It is even so. From the battlements of heaven the angels look down upon you, and they seem to cry to-day to you with sweet, silvery voice, "Ye shall reap if ye faint not; ye shall be rewarded if ye continue stedfast in the work and faith of Christ." And the saints look down upon you—Abraham, Isaac, and Jacob; martyrs and confessors, and your own pious relatives who have ascended to heaven, look down upon you, and if I might so speak, methinks sometimes you might hear the clapping of their hands when you have resisted temptation and overcome the enemy; and you might see their suspense when you are lagging in the course, and you might hear their friendly word of caution as they bid you gird up the loins of your mind, and lay aside every weight, and still speed forward, never resting to take your breath, never staying for a moment's ease till you have attained the flowery beds of heaven, where you may rest forever. And recollect, these are not the only eyes that are looking upon you. The whole world looks upon a Christian: he is the observed of all observers. In a Christian every fault is seen. A worldly man may commit a thousand faults, and nobody notices him; but let a Christian do so, and he will very soon have his faults published to the wide world. Everywhere men are looking at Christians. And it is quite right that they should do so. I remember a young man, a member of a Christian church, who went to a public-house hall of the lowest character; and he was no sooner mounting up the stairs, than one of them said, "Ah! here comes the Methodist; we will give it to him." As soon as they had him in the room, they first of all lead him up and down to let everybody see the Methodist who had come among them, and then they kicked him down stairs. I sent them my respectful compliments for doing so, for it served him right; and I took care that he was kicked down stairs in another sense afterwards, and kicked out of the church. The world would not have him and the church would not have him. The world then looks upon you, it never misses an opportunity of throwing your religion in your teeth. If you don't give sixteen ounces to the pound of morality, if you don't come up to the mark in everything, you will hear of it again. Don't think the world is ever asleep. We say, "as sound asleep as a church," and that is a very good proverb; but we cannot say, "as sound asleep as the world" for it never sleeps; it always has its eyes open, it is always watching us in all we do. The eyes of the world are upon you. "We are compassed about with a great cloud of witnesses;" "let us run with patience the race that is set before us." And there are darker and yet more malignant eyes that scowl upon us. There are spirits that people this air, who are under the prince of the power of the air, who watch every day for our halting.

> "Millions of spiritual creatures walk this earth,
> Both when we wake and when we sleep."

And alas! those spiritual creatures are not all good. There be those that are not yet chained and reserved in darkness, but who are permitted by God to wander through this world like roaring lions, seeking whom they may devour, ever ready to tempt us. And there is one at the head of them called Satan, *the enemy,* and you know his employment. He has access to the throne of God, and he makes most horrid use of it, for he accuses us day and night before the throne. The accuser of the brethren is not yet cast down—that is to be in the great day of the triumph of the Son of Man; but as Jesus stands our Advocate before the throne, so does old Satan first watch us and tempt us, and then stands as our accuser before the bar of God. O my dear brothers and sisters, if you have entered into this race, and have commenced it, let these many eyes urge you forward.

> "A cloud of witnesses around
> Hold thee in full survey;
> Forget the steps already trod,
> And onward urge thy way."

And now a more urgent consideration still. Recollect, your race is win or lose—death or life, hell or heaven, eternal misery or everlasting joy. What a stake that is for which you run. If I may so put it, you are running for your life; and if that does not make a man run nothing will. Put a man there on yonder hill, and put another after him with a drawn sword seeking his life, If there is any run in him you will soon see him run; there will be no need for us to shout out to him, "Run, man, run" for he is quite certain that his life is at hazard, and he speeds with all his might—speeds till the veins stand like whipcords on his brow, and a hot sweat runs from every pore of his body—and still flees onward. Now, he looks behind, and sees the avenger of blood speeding after him; he does not stop; he spurns the ground, and on he flees till he reaches the city of refuge, where he is safe. Ah! if we had eyes to see, and if we knew who it is that is pursuing us every afar of our lives, how we should run! for lo! O man, hell is behind thee, sin pursues thee, evil seeks to overtake thee; the City of Refuge has its gates wide open; I beseech thee, rest not till thou canst say with confidence, "I have entered into this rest, and now I am secure, I know that my Redeemer liveth." And rest not even then, for this is not the place for rest; rest not until thy six days work is done; and thy heavenly Sabbath is begun. Let this life be thy six days of ever-toiling faith. Obey thy Master's commandment; "labour therefore to enter into this rest," seeing that there are many who shall not enter in, because through their want of faith they shall not be able. If that urge not a man to speed forward, what can?

But let me picture yet one more thing; and may that help you onward! Christian, run onward, for remember *who it is that stands at the winning post.* You are to run onward, always looking unto Jesus, then Jesus must be at the end. We are always to be looking forward, and never backward; therefore Jesus must be there. Are you loitering? See him with his open wounds. Are you about to leave the course? See him with his bleeding hands; will not that constrain you to devote yourself to him? Will not that impel you to speed your course, and never loiter until you have obtained the crown? Your dying Master cries to you to-day, and he says. "By my agony and bloody sweat; by my cross and passion, onward! By my life, which I gave for you; by the death which I endured for your sake, onward!" And see! He holds out his hand, laden with a crown sparkling with many a star, and he says, "By this crown, onward!" I beseech you, onward, my beloved; press forward, for "I know that there is laid up for me a crown of life which fadeth not away, and not for me only, but for all them that love his appearing."

I have thus addressed myself to all sorts of characters. Will you this afternoon take that home to yourself which is the most applicable to your case. Those of you who make no profession of religion, are living without God and without Christ, strangers to the commonwealth of Israel,—let me affectionately remind you that the day is coming when you will want religion. It is very well now to be sailing over the smooth waters of life, but the rough billows of Jordan will make you want a Saviour. It is hard work to die without a hope; to take that last leap in the dark is a frightful thing indeed. I have seen the old man die when he has declared he would not die. He has stood upon the brink of death, and he has said, "All dark, dark, dark! O God, I cannot die." And his agony has been fearful when the strong hand of the destroyer has seemed to push him over the precipice. He lingered shivering on the brink, and feared to launch away." And frightful was the moment when the foot slipped and the solid earth was left, and the soul was sinking into the depths of eternal wrath. You will want a Saviour then, when your pulse is faint and few; you will need an angel then to stand at your bedside: and when the spirit is departing, you will need a sacred convoy to pilot you through the dark clouds of death and guide you through the iron gate, and lead you to the blessed mansion in the land of the hereafter. Oh, "seek ye the Lord while he may be found, call ye upon him while he is near: Let the wicked forsake his way, and the unrighteous man his thoughts: and let him return unto the Lord and he will have mercy upon him; and to our God, for he will abundantly pardon. For my thoughts are not your thoughts, neither are your ways my ways, saith the Lord. For as the heavens are higher than the earth, so are my ways higher than your ways, and my thoughts than your thoughts." O Lord, turn us and we shall be turned. Draw us and we will run after thee; and thine shall be the glory; for the crown of our race shall be cast at thy feet, and thou shalt have the glory forever and ever.

3

Heaven and Hell

"And I say unto you, That many shall come from the east and west, and shall sit down with Abraham, and Isaac, and Jacob, in the kingdom of heaven. But the children of the kingdom shall be cast out into outer darkness; there shall be weeping and gnashing of teeth."

—Matthew 8:11-12

THIS IS A LAND WHERE plain speaking is allowed, and where the people are willing to afford a fair hearing to any one who can tell them that which is worth their attention. To-night I am quite certain of an attentive audience, for I know you too well to suppose otherwise. This field, as you are all aware, is private property; and I would just give a suggestion to those who go out in the open air to preach—that it is far better to get into a field, or a plot of unoccupied building-ground, than to block up the roads and stop business; it is moreover, far better to be somewhat under protection, so that we can at once prevent disturbance.

To-night, I shall, I hope, encourage you to seek the road to heaven. I shall also have to utter some very sharp things concerning the end of the lost in the pit of hell. Upon both these subjects I will try and speak, as God helps me. But, I beseech you, as you love your souls, weigh right and wrong this night; see whether what I say be the truth of God. If it be not, reject it utterly, and cast it away; but if it is, at your peril disregard it; for, as you shall answer before God, the great Judge of heaven and earth, it will go ill with you if the words of his servant and of his Scripture be despised.

My text has two parts. The first is very agreeable to my mind, and gives me pleasure; the second is terrible in the extreme; but, since they are both the truth, they must be preached. The first part of my text is, "I say unto you, that many shall come from the east and west, and shall sit down with Abraham, and Isaac, and Jacob, in the kingdom of heaven." The sentence which I call the black, dark, and threatening part is this: "But the children of the kingdom shall be cast out into outer darkness: there shall be weeping and gnashing of teeth."

I. Let us take the first part. Here is a *most glorious promise.* I will read it again: "Many shall come from the east and west, and shall sit down with Abraham, and Isaac, and Jacob, in the kingdom of heaven." I like that text, because it tells me what heaven is, and gives me a beautiful picture of it. It says, it is a place where I shall sit down with Abraham, and Isaac, and Jacob. O what a sweet thought that is for the working man! He often wipes the hot sweat from his face, and he wonders whether there is a land where he shall have to toil no longer. He scarcely ever eats a mouthful of bread that is not moistened with the sweat of his brow. Often he comes home weary, and flings himself upon his couch, perhaps too tired to sleep. He says, "Oh! is there no land where I can rest? Is there no place where I can sit, and for once let these weary limbs be still? Is there no land where I can be quiet? Yes, thou son of toil and labor,

> "There is a happy land
> Far, far away—"

where toil and labor are unknown. Beyond yon blue welkin there is a city fair and bright, its walls are jasper, and its light is brighter than the sun. There "the weary are at rest, and the wicked cease from troubling." Immortal spirits are yonder, who never wipe sweat from their brow, for "they sow not, neither do they reap;" they have not to toil and labor.

> "There, on a green and flowery mount,
> Their weary souls shall sit;
> And with transporting joys recount
> The labors of their feet."

To my mind, one of the best views of heaven is, that *it is a land of rest*— especially to the working man. Those who have not to work hard, think they will love heaven as a place of service. That is very true. But to the working man, to the man who toils with his brain or with his hands, it must ever be a sweet thought that there is a land where we shall rest. Soon, this voice will never be strained again; soon, these lungs will never have to exert themselves beyond their power; soon, this brain shall not be racked for thought; but I shall sit at the banquet-table of God; yea, I shall recline on the bosom of Abraham, and be at ease for ever. Oh! weary sons and daughters of Adam, you will not have to drive the ploughshare into the unthankful soil in heaven, you will not need to rise to daily toils before the sun hath risen, and labor still when the sun hath long ago gone to his rest; but ye shall be still, ye shall be quiet, ye shall rest yourselves, for all are rich in heaven, all are happy there, all are peaceful. Toil, trouble, travail, and labor, are words that cannot be spelled in heaven; they have no such things there, for they always rest.

And mark the *good company they sit with.* They are to "sit down with Abraham, and Isaac, and Jacob." Some people think that in heaven we shall know nobody. But our text declares here, that we "shall sit down with Abraham, and Isaac, and Jacob." Then I am sure that we shall be aware that they are Abraham, and Isaac, and Jacob. I have heard of a good woman, who asked her husband, when she was dying, "My dear, do you think you will know me when you and I get to heaven?" "Shall I know you?" he said, "why, I have always known you while I have been here, and do you think I shall be a greater fool when I get to heaven?" I think it was a very good answer. If we have known one another here, we shall know one another there. I have dear departed friends up there, and it is always a sweet thought to me, that when I shall put my foot, as I hope I may, upon the threshold of heaven, there will come my sisters and brothers to clasp me by the hand and say, "Yes, thou loved one, and thou art here." Dear relatives that have been separated, you will meet again in heaven. One of you has lost a mother—she is gone above; and if you follow the track of Jesus, you shall meet her there. Methinks I see yet another coming to meet you at the door of Paradise; and though the ties of natural affection may be in a measure forgotten,—I may be allowed to use a figure—how blessed would she be as she turned to God, and said, "Here am I, and the children that thou hast given me." We shall recognize our friends:—husband, you will know your wife again. Mother, you will know those dear babes of yours—you marked their features when they lay panting and gasping for breath. You know how ye hung over their graves when the cold sod was sprinkled over them, and it was said, "Earth to earth. Dust to dust, and ashes to ashes." But ye shall hear those loved voices again: ye shall hear those sweet voices once more; ye shall yet know that those whom ye loved have been loved by God. Would not that be a dreary heaven for us to inhabit, where we should be alike unknowing and unknown? I would not care to go to such a heaven as that. I believe that heaven is a fellowship of the saints, and that we shall know one another there. I have often thought I should love to see Isaiah; and, as soon as I get to heaven, methinks, I would ask for him, because he spoke more of Jesus Christ than all the rest. I am sure I should want to find out good George Whitefield—he who so continually preached to the people, and wore himself out with a more than seraphic zeal. O yes! We shall have choice company in heaven when we get there. There will be no distinction of learned and unlearned, clergy and laity, but we shall walk freely one among another; we shall feel that we are brethren;

we shall "sit down with Abraham, and Isaac, and Jacob." I have heard of a lady who was visited by a minister on her deathbed, and she said to him, "I want to ask you one question, now I am about to die." "Well," said the minister, "what is it?" "Oh!" said she, in a very affected way, "I want to know if there are two places in heaven, because I could not bear that Betsy in the kitchen should be in heaven along with me, she is so unrefined?" The minister turned round and said, "O! don't trouble yourself about that, madam. There is no fear of that; for, until you get rid of you accursed pride, you will never enter heaven at all." We must all get rid of our pride. We must come down and stand on an equality in the sight of God, and see in every man a brother, before we can hope to be found in glory. Aye, we bless God, we thank him that there will be no separate table for one and for another. The Jew and the Gentile will sit down together. The great and the small shall feed in the same pasture, and we shall "sit down with Abraham, and Isaac, and Jacob, in the kingdom of heaven."

But my text hath a yet greater depth of sweetness, for it says, that "*many* shall come and shall sit down." Some narrow-minded bigots think that heaven will be a very small place, where there will be a very few people, who went to their chapel or their church. I confess, I have no wish for a very small heaven, and love to read in the Scriptures that there are many mansions in my Father's house. How often do I hear people say, "Ah! straight is the gate and narrow is the way, and few there be that find it. There will be very few in heaven; there will be most lost." My friend, I differ from you. Do you think that Christ will let the devil beat him? That he will let the devil have more in hell than there will be in heaven? No; it is impossible. For then Satan would laugh at Christ. There will be more in heaven than there are among the lost. God says, that "there will be a number that no man can number who will be saved;" but he never says, that there will be a number that no man can number that will be lost. There will be a host beyond all count who will get into heaven. What glad tidings for you and for me! For, if there are so many to be saved, why should not I be saved? Why should not you? Why should not yon man, over there in the crowd, say, "cannot I be one among the multitude?" And may not that poor woman there take heart, and say, "Well, if there were but half-a-dozen saved, I might fear that I should not be one; but, since many are to come, why should not I also be saved?" Cheer up, disconsolate! Cheer up, son of mourning, child of sorrow, there is hope for thee still! I can never know that any man is past God's grace. There be a few that have sinned that sin that is unto death, and God gives them up; but the vast host of mankind are yet within the reach of sovereign mercy—"and many of them shall come from the east and from the west, and shall sit down in the kingdom of heaven."

Look at my text again, and you will see where these people come from. They are to "come from the east and west." The Jews said that they would all come from Palestine, every one of them, every man, woman, and child; that there would not be one in heaven that was not a Jew. And the Pharisees thought that, if they were not all Pharisees, they could not be saved. But Jesus Christ said, there will be many that will come from the east and from the west. There will be a multitude from that far-off land of China, for God is doing a great work there, and we hope that the gospel will yet be victorious in that land. There will be a multitude from this western land of England, from the western country beyond the sea in America, and from the south in Australia, and from the north in Canada, Siberia, and Russia. From the uttermost parts of the earth there shall come many to sit down in the kingdom of God. But I do not think this text is to be understood so much geographically as spiritually. When it says that they "shall come from the east and west," I think it does not refer to nations particularly, but to different kinds of people. Now, "the east and the west" signify those who are the very farthest off from religion; yet many of them will be saved and get to heaven. There is a class of persons who will always be looked upon as hopeless. Many a time have I heard a man or woman say of such a one, "He cannot be saved: he is too abandoned. What is *he* good for? Ask *him* to go to a place of worship—he was drunk on Saturday night. What would be the use of reasoning with *him?* There is no hope for him. He is a hardened fellow. See what he has done these many years. What good will it be to speak to him? Now, hear this, ye who think your fellows worse than yourselves—ye who condemn others, whereas ye are often just as guilty: Jesus Christ says, "many shall come from the east and west." There will be many in heaven that were drunkards once. I believe, among that blood-bought throng, there are many who reeled in and out the tavern half their lifetime. But, by the power of divine grace, they were able to dash the liquor-cup to the ground. They renounced the riot of intoxication—fled away from it—and served God. Yes! There will be many in heaven who were drunkards on earth. There will be many harlots: some of the most abandoned will be found there. You remember the story of Whitefield's once saying, that there would be some in heaven who were "the devil's castaways;" some that the devil would hardly think good enough for him, and yet whom Christ would save. Lady Huntingdon once gently hinted that such language was not quite proper. But, just at the time, there happened to be heard a ring at the bell, and Whitefield went down-stairs. Afterwards he came up and said, "Your ladyship, what do you think a poor woman had to say to me just now? She was a sad profligate, and she said, 'O, Mr. Whitefield, when you were preaching, you told us that Christ would take in the devil's castaways, and I am one of them,'" and that was the means of her salvation. Shall anybody ever check us from preaching to the lowest of the low? I have been accused of getting all the rabble of London around me. God bless the rabble! God save the rabble! Then, say I: But, suppose they are "the rabble," who need the gospel more than they do? Who require to have Christ preached to them more than they do? We have lots of those who preach to ladies and gentlemen, and we want some one to preach to the rabble in these degenerate days. Oh! here is comfort for me, for many of the rabble are to come from the east and from the west. Oh! what would you think if you were to see the difference between some that are in heaven and some that shall be there? There might be found one whose hair hangs across his eyes, his locks are matted, he looks horrible, his bloated eyes start from his face, he grins almost like an idiot, he has drunk away his very brain until life seems to have departed, so far as sense and being are concerned; yet I would tell to you, "that man is capable of salvation:—and in a few years I might say "look up yonder;" see you that bright star? discern you that man with a crown of pure gold upon his head? do you notice that being clad in robes of sapphire and in garments of light? That is the self-same man who sat there a poor, benighted, almost idiotic being; yet sovereign grace and mercy have saved him! There are none, except those, as I have said before, who have sinned the unpardonable sin, who are beyond God's mercy. Fetch me out the worst, and still I would preach the gospel to them; fetch me out the vilest, still I would preach to them, because I recollect my Master said, "Go ye out into the highways and hedges, and compel them to come in that my house may be filled." "Many shall come from the east and west, and shall sit down with Abraham, and Isaac, and Jacob, in the kingdom of heaven."

There is one more word I must notice before I have done with this sweet portion—that is the word *"shall."* Oh! I love God's "shalls" and "wills." There is nothing comparable to them. Let a man say "shall," what is it good for? "I will," says man, and he never performs; "I shall," says he, and he breaks his promise. But it is never so with God's "shalls." If he says "shall," it shall be; when he says "will," it will be. Now he has said here, "many *shall* come." The devil says "they shall not come;" but "they shall come." Their sins say "you can't come;" God says "you shall come." You, yourselves, say, "you won't come;" God says "you shall come." Yes! There are some here who are laughing at salvation, who can scoff at Christ and mock at the gospel; but I tell you some of you shall come yet. "What!" you say, "can God make me become a Christian?" I tell you yes, for herein rests the power of the gospel. It does not ask you consent; but it gets it. It does not say, Will you have it? But it makes you willing in the day of God's power. Not against your will, but it makes you willing. It shows you its value, and then you fall in love with it; and straightway you run after it and have it. Many people have said, "we will not have anything to do with religion." yet they have been converted. I have heard of a man who once went to chapel to hear the singing, and as soon as the minister began to preach, he put his fingers in his ears and would not listen. But by-and-by some tiny insect settled on his face, so that he was obliged to take one finger out of his ears to brush it away. Just then the minister said, "he that hath ears to hear let him hear." The man listened; and God met with him at that moment to his soul's conversion. He went out a new man, a changed character. He who came in to laugh retired to pray; he who came in to mock went out to bend his knee in penitence; he who entered to spend an idle hour went home to spend an hour in devotion with his God. The sinner became a saint; the profligate became a penitent. Who know that there may not be some like that here? The gospel wants not your consent, it gets it. It knocks the enmity out of your heart. You say, "I do not want to be saved;" Christ says you shall be. He makes your will turn round, and then you cry, "Lord, save, or I perish." "Ah," might Heaven exclaim, "I knew I would make you say that;" and then he rejoices over you because he has changed your will and made you willing in the day of his power. If Jesus Christ were to stand on the platform to-night, what would many people do with him? "O!" say some, "we would make him a King." I do not believe it. They would crucify him again, if they had the opportunity. If he were to come and say, "Here I am, I love you, will you be saved by me?" not one of you would consent if you were left to your will. If he should look upon you with those eyes, before whose power the lion would have crouched; if he spoke with that voice which poured forth a cataract of eloquence like a stream of nectar rolling down from the cliffs above, not a single person would come to be his disciple. No; it wants the power of the Spirit to make men come to Jesus Christ. He himself said, "No man can come to me except the Father who hath sent me draw him." Ah! we want that; and here we have it. They shall come! They shall come! Ye may laugh, ye may despise us; but Jesus Christ shall not die for nothing. If some of you reject him, there are some that will not. It there are some that are not saved, others *shall* be. Christ *shall* see his seed, he *shall* prolong his days, and the pleasure of the Lord *shall* prosper in his hands. Some think that Christ died, and yet, that some for whom he died will be lost. I never could understand that doctrine. If Jesus, my surety, bore my griefs and carried my sorrows, I believe myself to be as secure as the angels in heaven. God cannot ask payment twice. If Christ paid my debt, shall I have to pay it again? No.

> "Free from sin I walk at large
> The Saviour's blood's my full discharge;
> At his dear feet content I lay,
> A sinner saved, and homage pay."

They shall come! They shall come! And naught in heaven, nor on earth, nor in hell, can stop them from coming.

And now, thou chief of sinners, list one moment, while I call thee to Jesus. There is one person here to-night, who thinks himself the worst soul that ever lived. There is one who says to himself, "I do not deserve to be called to Christ, I am sure!" Soul! I call thee! thou lost, most wretched outcast, this night, by authority given me of God, I call thee to come to my Saviour. Some time ago, when I went into the County Court to see what they were doing, I heard a man's name called out, and immediately the man said, "Make way! make way! They call me!" And up he came. Now, I call the chief of sinners to-night, and let him say, "Make way! make way, doubts! make way, fears! make way, sins! Christ calls me! And if Christ calls me, that is enough!"

> "I'll to his gracious feet approach,
> Whose sceptre mercy gives.
> Perhaps he may command me, 'Touch!'
> And then the suppliant lives."

> "I can but perish if I go;
> I am resolved to try,
> For if I stay away, I know
> I must for ever die."

> "But, should I die with mercies sought,
> When I the king have tried,
> That were to die, (delightful thought!)
> As sinner never died."

Go and try my Saviour! Go and try my Saviour! If he cast you away after you have sought him, tell in the pit that Christ would not hear you. But *that* you shall never be allowed to do. It would dishonor the mercy of the covenant for God to cast away one penitent sinner; and it never shall be while it is written, "Many shall come from the east and west, and shall sit down with Abraham, and Isaac, and Jacob, in the kingdom of heaven."

II. The second part of my text is heart-breaking. I could preach with great delight to myself from the first part; but here is a dreary task to my soul, because there are gloomy words here. But, as I have told you, what is written in the Bible must be preached, whether it be gloomy or cheerful. There are some ministers who never mention anything about hell. I heard of a minister who once said to his congregation, "If you do not love the Lord Jesus Christ, you will be sent to that place which it is not polite to mention." He ought not to have been allowed to preach again, I am sure, if he could not use plain words. Now, if I saw that house on fire over there, do you think I would stand and say, "I believe the operation of combustion is proceeding yonder?" No; I would call out, "Fire! fire! and then everybody would know what I meant. So, if the Bible says, "The children of the kingdom shall be cast out into outer darkness," am I to stand here and mince the matter at all? God forbid! We must speak the truth as it is written. It is a terrible truth, for it says, *"the children of the kingdom* shall be cast out!" Now, who are those children? I will tell you. "The children of the kingdom" are those people who are noted for the externals of piety, but who have nothing of the internals of it. People whom you will see with their Bibles and Hymn Books marching off to chapel as religiously as possible, or going to church as devoutly and demurely as they can, looking as sombre and serious as parish beadles, and fancying that they are quite sure to be saved, though their hearts are not in the matter; nothing but their bodies. These are the persons who are "the children of the kingdom." They have no grace, no life, no Christ, and they shall be cast into outer darkness.

Again, these people are *the children of pious fathers and mothers.* There is nothing touches a man's heart, mark you, like talking about his mother. I have heard of a swearing sailor, whom nobody could manage, not even the police, who was always making some disturbance wherever he went. Once he went into a place of worship, and no one could keep him still; but a gentleman went up and said to him, "Jack, you had a mother once." With that the tears ran down his cheeks. He said, "Ha! bless you, sir, I had; and I brought her gray hairs with sorrow to the grave, and a pretty fellow I am to be here to-night." He then sat down, quite sobered and subdued by the very mention of

43

his mother. Ah, and there are some of you, "children of the kingdom," who can remember your mothers. Your mother took you on her knee and taught you early to pray; your father tutored you in the ways of godliness. And yet you are here to-night, without grace in you heart—without hope of heaven. You are going downwards towards hell as fast as your feet can carry you. There are some of you who have broken your poor mother's heart. Oh! if I could tell you what she has suffered for you when you have at night been indulging in you sin. Do you know what your guilt will be, ye "children of the kingdom," if ye perish after a pious mother's prayers and tears have fallen upon you? I can conceive of no one entering hell with a worse grace than the man who goes there with drops of his mother's tears on his head, and with his father's prayers following him at his heels. Some of you will inevitably endure this doom; some of you, young men and women, shall wake up one day and find yourselves in utter darkness, while your parents shall be up there in heaven, looking down upon you with upbraiding eyes, seeming to say, "What! after all we did for you, all we said, are ye come to this?" "Children of the kingdom!" do not think that a pious mother can save you. Do not think, because your father was a member of such-and-such a church, that his godliness will save you. I can suppose some one standing at heaven's gate, and demanding, "Let me in! Let me in!" What for? "Because my mother is in there." Your mother had nothing to do with you. If she was holy, she was holy for herself; if she was evil, she was evil for herself. "But my grandfather prayed for me!" That is no use: did you pray for yourself? "No, I did not." Then grandfather's prayers, and grandmother's prayers, and father's and mother's prayers may be piled on the top of one another till they reach the stars, but they never can make a ladder for you to go to heaven by. You must seek God for yourself; or rather, God must seek you. You must have vital experience of godliness in you heart, or else you are lost, even though all your friends were in heaven. That was a dreadful dream which a pious mother once had, and told to her children. She thought the judgment day was come. The great books were opened. They all stood before God. And Jesus Christ said, "Separate the chaff from the wheat; put the goats on the left hand, and the sheep on the right. The mother dreamed that she and her children were standing just in the middle of the great assembly. And the angel came, and said, "I must take the mother, she is a sheep: she must go to the right hand. The children are goats: they must go on the left." She thought as she went, her children clutched her, and said, "Mother, can we part? Must we be separated?" She then put her arms around them, and seemed to say, "My children, I would, if possible, take you with me." But in a moment the angel touched her; her cheeks were dried, and now, overcoming natural affection, being rendered supernatural and sublime, resigned to God's will, she said, "My children, I taught you well, I trained you up, and you forsook the ways of God; and now all I have to say is, Amen to you condemnation." Thereupon they were snatched away, and she saw them in perpetual torment while she was in heaven. Young man, what will you think, when the last day comes, to hear Christ say, "Depart, ye cursed?" And there will be a voice just behind him, saying, Amen. And, as you inquire whence came the voice, you will find it was your mother. Or, young woman, when thou art cast away into utter darkness, what will you think to hear a voice saying, Amen. And as you look, there sits your father, his lips still moving with the solemn curse. Ah! "children of the kingdom," the penitent reprobates will enter heaven, many of them; publicans and sinners will get there; repenting drunkards and swearers will be saved; but many of the "children of the kingdom" will be cast out. Oh! to think that you who have been so well trained should be lost, while many of the worse will be saved. It will be the hell of hells for you to look up and see there "poor Jack," the drunkard, lying in Abraham's bosom, while you, who have had a pious mother, are cast into hell, simply because you would not believe on the Lord Jesus Christ, but put his gospel from you, and lived and died without it! That were the very sting of all, to see ourselves cast away, when the chief of sinners finds salvation.

Now list to me a little while—I will not detain you long—whilst I undertake the doleful task of telling you what is to become of these "children of the kingdom." Jesus Christ says they are to be "cast into utter darkness, where there is weeping and gnashing of teeth."

First, notice, they are to be *cast out*. They are not said to *go;* but, when they come to heaven's gates, they are to be *cast* out. As soon as hypocrites arrive at the gates of heaven, Justice will say, "There he comes! there he comes! He spurned a father's prayers, and mocked a mother's tears. He has forced his way downward against all the advantages mercy has supplied. And now, there he comes. "Gabriel, take the man." The angel, binding you hand and foot, holds you one single moment over the mouth of the chasm. He bids you look down—down—down. There is no bottom; and you hear coming up from the abyss, sullen moans, and hollow groans, and screams of tortured ghosts. You quiver, your bones melt like wax, and your marrow quakes within you. Where is now thy might? and where thy boasting and bragging? Ye shriek and cry, ye beg for mercy; but the angel, with one tremendous grasp, seizes you fast, and then hurls you down, with the cry, "Away, away!" And down you go to the pit that is bottomless, and roll for

45

ever downward—downward—downward—ne'er to find a resting-place for the soles of your feet. Ye shall be cast out.

And *where are you to be cast to?* Ye are to be cast "into outer darkness;" ye are to be put in the place where there will be no hope. For, by "light," in Scripture, we understand "hope;" and you are to be put "into outer darkness," where there is no light—no hope. Is there a man here who has no hope? I cannot suppose such a person. One of you, perhaps, says, "I am thirty pounds in debt, and shall be sold up by-and-by; but I have a hope that I may get a loan, and so escape my difficulty." Says another, "My business is ruined, but things may take a turn yet—I have a hope." Says another, "I am in great distress, but I hope that God will provide for me." Another says, "I am fifty pounds in debt; I am sorry for it; but I will set these strong hands to work, and do my best to get out of it." One of you thinks a friend is dying, but you have a hope that, perhaps, the fever may take a turn—that he may yet live. But, in hell, there is no hope. They have not even the hope of dying—the hope of being annihilated. They are for ever—for ever—for ever—lost! On every chain in hell, there is written "for ever." In the fires, there blaze out the words, "for ever." Up above their heads, they read "for ever." Their eyes are galled, and their hearts are pained with the thought that it is "for ever." Oh! if I could tell you to-night that hell would one day be burned out, and that those who were lost might be saved, there would be a jubilee in hell at the very thought of it. But it cannot be—it is *"for ever"* they are "cast into utter darkness."

But I want to get over this as quickly as I can; for who can bear to talk thus to his fellow-creatures? What is it that the lost are doing? They are "weeping and gnashing their teeth." Do you gnash you teeth now? You would not do it except you were in pain and agony. Well, in hell there is always gnashing of teeth. And do you know why? There is one gnashing his teeth at his companion, and mutters, "I was led into hell by you; you led me astray, you taught me to drink the first time." And the other gnashes his teeth and says, "What if I did? You made me worse than I should have been in after times." There is a child who looks at her mother, and says, "Mother, you trained me up to vice." And the mother gnashes her teeth again at the child, and says, "I have no pity for you, for you excelled me in it, and led me into deeper sin." Fathers gnash their teeth at their sons, and sons at their fathers. And, methinks, if there are any who will have to gnash their teeth more than others, it will be seducers, when they see those whom they have led from the paths of virtue, and hear them saying, "Ah! we are glad you are in hell with us, you deserve it, for you led us here." Have any of you, to-night, upon your consciences the fact that you have led others to the pit? O, may sovereign grace forgive you. "We have gone astray like lost sheep," said David. Now a lost sheep never goes astray alone, if it is one of a flock. I lately read of a sheep that leaped over the parapet of a bridge, and was followed by every one of the flock. So, if one man goes astray, he leads others with him. Some of you will have to account for others' sins when you get to hell, as well as your own. Oh, what "weeping and gnashing of teeth" there will be in that pit!

Now shut the black book. Who wants to say any more about it? I have warned you solemnly. I have told you of the wrath to come. The evening darkens, and the sun is setting. Ah! and the evenings darken with some of you. I can see gray-headed men here. Are your gray hairs a crown of glory, or a fool's cap to you? Are you on the very verge of heaven, or are you tottering on the brink of your grave, and sinking down to perdition?

Let me warn you, gray-headed men; your evening is coming. O, poor, tottering gray-head, wilt thou take the last step into the pit? Let a young child step before thee, and beg thee to consider. There is thy staff—it has nothing of earth to rest upon: and now, ere thou diest, bethink thyself this night; let seventy years of sin start up; let the ghosts of thy forgotten transgressions march before thine eyes. What wilt thou do with seventy wasted years to answer for—with seventy years of criminality to bring before God? God give thee grace this night to repent and to put thy trust in Jesus.

And you, middle-aged men, are not safe; the evening lowers with you, too; you may soon die. A few mornings ago, I was roused early from my bed, by the request that I would hasten to see a dying man. I hurried off with all speed to see the poor creature; but when I reached the house, he was dead—a corpse. As I stood in the room I thought, "Ah! that man little thought he should die so soon." There were his wife and children, and friends—they little thought he would die; for he was hale, strong, and hearty but a few days before. None of you have a lease of your lives. If you have, where is it? Go and see if you have it anywhere in your chest at home. No! ye may die to-morrow. Let me therefore warn you by the mercy of God; let me speak to you as a brother may speak; for I love you, you know I do, and would press the matter home to your hearts. Oh, to be amongst the many who shall be accepted in Christ—how blessed that will be! and God has said that whosoever shall call on his name shall be saved: he casts out none that come unto him through Christ.

And now, ye youths and maidens, one word with you. Perhaps you think that religion is not for you. "Let us be happy," say you: "let us be merry and joyous." How long, young man, how long? "Till I am twenty-one." Are you sure that you will live till then? Let me tell you one thing. If you do live till that time, if you have no heart for God now, you will have none then. Men do not get better if left alone. It is with them as with the garden: if you let it alone, and permit weeds to grow, you will not expect to find it better in six months—but worse. Ah! men talk as if they could repent when they like. It is the work of God to give us repentance. Some even say, "I shall turn to God on such-and-such a day. Ah! if you felt aright, you would say, "I must run to God, and ask him to give me repentance now, lest I should die before I have found Jesus Christ, my Saviour."

Now, one word in conclusion. I have told you of heaven and hell; what is the way, then, to escape from hell and to be found in heaven? I will not tell you my old tale again to-night. I recollect when I told it you before, a good friend in the crowd said, "Tell us something fresh, old fellow." Now really, in preaching ten times a week, we cannot always say things fresh. You have heard John Gough, and you know he tells his tales over again. I have nothing but the old gospel. "He that believeth and is baptized shall be saved." There is nothing here of works. It does not say, "He who is a good man shall be saved," but "he who believes and is baptized." Well, what is it to believe? It is to put your trust entirely upon Jesus. Poor Peter once believed, and Jesus Christ said to him, "Come on, Peter, walk to me on the water." Peter went stepping along on the tops of the waves without sinking; but when he looked at the waves, he began to tremble, and down he went. Now, poor sinner, Christ says, "Come on; walk on your sins; come to me; and if you do, he will give you power. If you believe on Christ, you will be able to walk over your sins—to tread upon them and overcome them. I can remember the time when my sins first stared me in the face. I thought myself the most accursed of all men. I had not committed any very great open transgressions against God; but I recollected that I had been well trained and tutored, and I thought my sins were thus greater than other people's. I cried to God to have mercy; and I feared that he would not pardon me. Month after month, I cried to God, and he did not hear me, and I knew not what it was to be saved. Sometimes I was so weary of the world that I desired to die; but then I recollected that there was a worse world after this, and that it would be an ill matter to rush before my Maker unprepared. At times I wickedly thought God a most heartless tyrant, because he did not answer my prayer; and then, at others, I thought, "I deserve his displeasure; if he sends me to hell, he will be just." But I remember the hour when I stepped into a little place of worship, and saw a tall, thin man step into the pulpit: I have never seen him from that day, and probably never shall, till we meet in heaven. He opened the Bible and read, with a feeble voice, "Look unto me, and be ye saved all the ends of the earth; for I am God, and beside me there is none else." Ah, thought I, I am one of the ends of the earth; and then turning round, and fixing his gaze on me, as if he knew me, the minister said, "Look, look, look." Why, I thought I had a great deal to *do*, but I found it was only to *look*. I thought I had a garment to spin out for myself; but I found that if I looked, Christ would give me a garment. Look, sinner, that is to be saved. Look unto him, all ye ends of the earth, and be saved. That is what the Jews did, when Moses held up the brazen serpent. He said, "Look!" and they looked. The serpent might be twisting round them, and they might be nearly dead; but they simply looked, and the moment they looked, the serpent dropped off, and they were healed. Look to Jesus, sinner. "None but Jesus can do helpless sinners good." There is a hymn we often sing, but which I do not think is quite right. It says,

"Venture on him, venture wholly;
    Let no other trust intrude."

Now, it is no venture to trust in Christ, not in the least; he who trusts in Christ is quite secure. I recollect that, when dear John Hyatt was dying, Matthew Wilks said to him, in his usual tone, "Well, John, could you trust your soul in the hands of Jesus Christ now?" "Yes," said he, "a million! a million souls!" I am sure that every Christian that has ever trusted in Christ can say Amen to that. Trust in him; he will never deceive you. My blessed Master will never cast you away.

I cannot speak much longer, and I have only to thank you for your kindness. I never saw so large a number so still and quiet. I do really think, after all the hard things that have been said, that the English people know who loves them, and that they will stand by the man who stands by them. I thank every one of you; and above all, I beg you, if there be reason or sense in what I have said, bethink yourselves of what you are, and may the Blessed Spirit reveal to you your state! May he show you that you are dead, that you are lost, ruined. May he make you feel what a dreadful thing it would be to sink into hell! May he point you to heaven! May he take you as the angel did of old, and put his hand upon you, and say, "Flee! flee! flee! Look to the mountain; look not behind thee; stay not in all the plain." And may we all meet in heaven at last; and there we shall be happy for ever.

4

Heaven

"As it is written, Eye hath not seen, nor ear heard, neither have entered into the heart of man, the things which God hath prepared for them that love him. But God hath revealed them unto us by his Spirit; for the Spirit searcheth all things, yea, the deep things of God."

—1 Corinthians 2:9-10

HOW VERY FREQUENTLY VERSES OF Scripture are misquoted! Instead of turning to the Bible, to see how it is written, and saying, "How readest thou?" we quote from one another; and thus a passage of Scripture is handed down misquoted, by a king of tradition, from father to son, and passes as current among a great number of Christian persons. How very frequently at our prayer meetings do we hear our brethren describing heaven as a place of which we cannot conceive! They say, "Eye hath not seen, nor ear heard, neither have entered into the heart of man, the things which God hath prepared for them that love him;" and there they stop, not seeing that the very marrow of the whole passage lies in this—"But God hath revealed them unto us by his Spirit." So that the joys of heaven (if this passage alludes to heaven, which, I take it, is not quite so clear as some would suppose), are, after all, not things of which we cannot conceive; for "God hath revealed them unto us by his Spirit."

I have hinted that this passage is most commonly applied to heaven, and I shall myself also so apply it in some measure, this morning. But any one who reads the connexion will discover that the apostle is not talking about heaven at all. He is only speaking of this—that the wisdom of this world is not able to discover the things of God—that the merely carnal mind is not able to know the deep spiritual things of our most holy religion. He says, "We speak the wisdom of God in a mystery, even the hidden wisdom, which God ordained before the world unto our glory: Which none of the princes of this world knew: for had they known it, they would not have crucified the Lord of glory. But as it is written, Eye hath not seen, nor ear heard, neither have entered into the heart of man, the things which God hath prepared for them that love him. But God hath revealed them unto us by his Spirit; for the Spirit searcheth all things, yea, the deep things of God." And then he goes on lower down to say, "But the natural man receiveth not the things of the Spirit of God: for they are foolishness unto him: neither can he know them, because they are spiritually discerned." I take it, that this text is a great general fact, capable of specific application to certain cases; and that the great fact is this—that the things of God cannot be perceived by eye, and ear, and heart, but must be revealed by the Spirit of God; as they are unto all true believers. We shall take that thought, and endeavour to expand it this morning, explaining it concerning heaven, as well as regards other heavenly matters.

Every prophet who has stood upon the borders of a new dispensation might have uttered these words with peculiar force. He might have said, as he looked forward to the future, God having touched his eye with the anointing eye-salve of the Holy Spirit, "Eye hath not seen, nor ear heard, neither have entered into the heart of man, the things that God hath prepared for them that love him; but God hath revealed them unto us by his Spirit." We will divide the economy of free grace into different dispensations. We commence with the *patriarchal*. A patriarch, who like Abraham was gifted with foresight, might have looked forward to the Levitical dispensation, glorious with its tabernacle, its Shekinah, its gorgeous veil, its blazing altars; he might have caught a glimpse of Solomon's magnificent temple, and even by anticipation heard the sacred song ascending from the assembled thousands of Jerusalem; he might have seen king Solomon upon his throne, surrounded with all his riches, and the people resting in peace and tranquillity in the promised land; and he might have turned to his brethren who lived in the patriarchal age, and said, "'Eye hath not seen, nor ear heard, neither have entered the heart of man, the things which God hath prepared for them that love him' in the next dispensation. Ye know not how clearly God will reveal himself in the Paschal Lamb—how sweetly the people will be led, and fed, and guided, and directed all the way through the wilderness—what a sweet and fair country it is that they shall inhabit; Eye hath not seen the brooks that gush with milk, nor the rivers that run with honey; ear hath not heard the melodious voices of the daughters of Shiloh, nor have entered into the heart of man the joys of the men of Zion, 'but God hath revealed them unto us by his Spirit.'"

And so, moreover, at the close of the Levitical dispensation, the *prophets* might have thus foretold the coming glories. Old Isaiah, standing in the midst of the temple, beholding its sacrifices, and the dim smoke that went up from them, when his eyes were opened by the Spirit of God, said—"Eye hath not seen, nor ear heard, neither have entered the heart of man, the things which God hath prepared for him that love him." He saw by faith Christ

51

crucified upon the cross; he beheld him weltering in his own blood in Gethsemane's garden; he saw the disciples going out of Jerusalem, to preach everywhere the Word of God; he marked the progress of Messiah's kingdom, and he looked down to these latter days, when every man under his own vine and fig tree doth worship God, none daring to make him afraid; and he could well have cheered the captives in Babylon in words like these,—"Now ye sit down and weep, and ye will not sing in a strange land the songs of Zion; but lift up your heads, for your salvation draweth nigh. Your eye hath not seen, nor your ear heard, the things which God hath prepared for them that love him; but he hath revealed them unto me by his Spirit." And now, beloved, we stand on the borders of a new era. The mediatorial dispensation is almost finished. In a few more years, if prophecy be not thoroughly misinterpreted, we shall enter upon another condition. This poor earth of ours, which has been swathed in darkness, shall put on her garments of light. She hath toiled a long while in travail and sorrow. Soon shall her groanings end. Her surface, which has been stained with blood, is soon to be purified by love, and a religion of peace is to be established. The hour is coming, when storms shall be hushed, when tempests shall be unknown, when whirlwind and hurricane shall stay their mighty force, and when "the kingdoms of this world shall become the kingdoms of our Lord and of his Christ." But you ask me what sort of kingdom that is to be, and whether I can show you any likeness thereof. I answer, no; "Eye hath not seen, nor ear heard, neither have entered the heart of man, the things which God hath prepared for them that love him," in the next, the millenial dispensation; "But God hath revealed them unto us by his Spirit." Sometimes, when we climb upwards, there are moments of contemplation when we can understand that verse, "From whence we look for the coming of our Lord Jesus Christ, who shall be revealed from heaven," and can anticipate that thrice blessed hour, when the King of kings shall put on his head the crown of the universe, when he shall gather up sheaves of sceptres, and put them beneath his arm—when he shall take the crowns from the heads of all monarchs, and welding them into one, shall put them on his own head, admist the shouts of ten thousand times ten thousand who shall chaunt his high praises. But it is little enough that we can guess of its wonders.

But persons are curious to know what kind of dispensation the Millennial one is to be. Will the temple, they ask, be erected in Jerusalem? Will the Jews be positively restored to their own land? Will the different nations all speak one language? Will they all resort to one temple? and ten thousand other questions. Beloved, we cannot answer you. "Eye hath not seen, nor ear heard, neither have entered the heart of man, the things which God hath prepared for them that love him." We do not profess to understand the minutiae of these things. It is enough for us to believe that a latter-day glory is approaching. Our eyes glisten with joy, in the full belief that it is coming; and our hearts swell big at the thought that our Master is to reign over the wide, wide world, and to win it for himself. But if you begin questioning us, we tell you that we cannot explain it. Just as under the legal dispensation there were types and shadows, but the mass of the people never saw Christ in them, so there are a great many different things in this dispensation which are types of the next, which will never be explained till we have more wisdom, more light, and more instruction. Just as the enlightened Jew partially foresaw what the Gospel was to be by the law, so may we guess the Millennium by the present, but we have not light enough: there are few who are taught enough in the deep things of God to explain them fully. Therefore we still say of the mass of mankind—"Eye hath not seen, nor ear heard, neither have entered the heart of man, things which God hath prepared for them that love him. But God hath revealed them *unto us* by his Spirit," in some measure, and he will do so more and more, by-and-bye.

And this brings us to make the application of the subject to *heaven itself*. You see, while it does not expressly mean heaven here, you may very easily bring it to bear upon it; for concerning heaven, unto which believers are all fast going, we may say "Eye hath not seen, nor ear heard, neither have entered the heart of man, the things which God hath prepared for them that love him. But God hath revealed them unto us by his Spirit."

Now, beloved, I am about to talk of heaven for this reason: you know, I never preach any funeral sermons for anybody, and never intend. I have passed by many persons who have died in our church, without having made any parade of funeral sermons; but, nevertheless, three or four of our friends having departed recently, I think I may speak a little to you about heaven, in order to cheer you, and God may thus bless their departure. It is to be no funeral sermon, however—no eulogium on the dead, and no oration pronounced over the departed. Frequent funeral sermons I utterly abhor, and I believe they are not under God's sanction and approval. Of the dead we should say nothing but that which is good: and in the pulpit we should say very little of that, except, perhaps, in the case of some very eminent saint; and then we should say very little of the man; but let the "honour be unto him that sitteth upon the throne, and unto the Lamb for ever."

Heaven—then, what is it? First, what is it not? *It is not a heaven of the* SENSES—"Eye hath not seen it." What glorious things the eye hath seen!

53

Have we not seen the gaudy pageantry of pomp crowding the gay streets. We have seen the procession of kings and princes; our eyes have been feasted with the display of glittering uniforms, of lavished gold and jewels, of chariots and of horses; and we have perhaps thought that the procession of the saints of God may be dimly shadowed forth thereby. But, oh it was but the thought of our poor infant mind, and far enough from the great reality. We may hear of the magnificence of the old Persian princes, of palaces covered with gold and silver, and floors inlaid with jewels; but we cannot thence gather a thought of heaven, for "eye hath not seen" it. We have thought, however, when we have come to the works of God, and our eye hath rested on them: surely we can get some glimpse of what heaven is here. By night we have turned our eye up to the blue azure, and we have seen the stars—those golden-fleeced sheep of God, feeding on the blue meadow of the sky, and we have said, "See! those are the nails in the floor of heaven up yonder;" and if this earth has such a glorious covering, what must that of the kingdom of heaven be? And when our eye has wandered from star to star, we have thought, "Now I can tell what heaven is by the beauty of its floor." But it is all a mistake. All that we can see can never help us to understand heaven. At another time we have seen some glorious landscape; we have seen the white river winding among the verdant fields like a stream silver, covered on either side with emerald; we have seen the mountain towering to the sky, the mist rising on it, or the golden sunrise covering all the east with glory; or we have seen the west, again, reddened with the light of the sun as it departed; and we have said, "Surely, these grandeurs must be something like heaven; we have clapped our hands, and exclaimed—

"Sweet fields beyond the swelling flood,
Stand dressed in living green."

We have imagined that there really were fields in heaven, and that things of earth were patterns of things in heaven. It was all a mistake:—"Eye hath not seen" it.

Equally does our text assert that "the ear hath not heard" it. Oh! have we not on the Sabbath day sometimes heard the sweet voice of the messenger of God, when he has by the Spirit spoken to our souls! We knew something of heaven then, we thought. At other times we have been entranced with the voice of the preacher, and with the remarkable sayings which he has uttered; we have been charmed by his eloquence; some of us have known what it is to sit and weep and smile alternately, under the power

54

of some mighty man who played with us as skilfully as David could have played on his harp; and we have said, "How sweet to hear those sounds! How glorious his eloquence! How wonderful his power of oratory! Now I think I know something of what heaven is, for my mind is so carried away, my passions are so excited, my imagination is so elevated, all the powers of my mind are stirred upon so that I can think of nothing but of what the preacher is speaking about!" But the ear is not the medium by which you can guess anything of heaven. The "ear hath not heard" it. At other times perhaps you have heard sweet music; and hath not music poured from the lungs of man— that noblest instrument in the world—or from some manufacture of harmony, and we have thought, "Oh! how glorious this is!" and fancied, "This is what John meant in the Revelation—'I heard a voice like many waters, and like exceeding great thunders, and I heard the voice of harpers harping with their harps;' and this must be something like heaven, something like the hallelujahs of the glorified." But ah! beloved, we made a mistake. "Ear hath not heard" it.

Here has been the very ground of that error into which many persons have fallen concerning heaven. They have said that they would like to go to heaven. What for? For this reason: *they looked upon it as a place where they should be free from bodily pain.* They should not have the head-ache or the tooth-ache there, nor any of those diseases which flesh is heir to, and whenever God laid his hand upon them they began to wish themselves in heaven, because they regarded it as a heaven of the senses—a heaven which the eye hath seen or the ear heard. A great mistake; for although we shall have a body free from pain, yet it is not a heaven where our senses shall indulge themselves. The labourer will have it, that heaven is a place,

> Where on a green and flowery mount
> His weary soul shall sit.

Another will have it that heaven is a place where he shall *eat to the full, and his body shall be satisfied.* We may use these as figures; but we are so degenerate that we are apt to build a fine Mahometan heaven, and to think, there shall we have all the delights of the flesh; there shall we drink from bowls of nectared wine; there shall we lavishly indulge ourselves, and our body shall enjoy every delight of which it is capable. What a mistake for us to conceive such a thing! Heaven is not a place for the delight of mere sense; we shall be raised not a sensual body, but a spiritual body. We can get no conceptions of heaven through the senses; they must always come through the Spirit. That is our first thought. It is not a heaven to be grasped by the senses.

But, secondly, *it is not a heaven of the* IMAGINATION. Poets let their imaginations fly with loosened wings, when they commence speaking of heaven. And how glorious are their descriptions of it! When we have read them, we say, "And is that heaven? I wish I was there." And we think we have some idea of heaven by reading books of poetry. Perhaps the preacher weaves the filigree work of fancy, and builds up in a moment by his words charming palaces, the tops of which are covered with gold, and the walls are ivory. He pictures to you lights brighter than the sun; a place where spirits flap their bright wings, where comets flash through the sky. He tells you of fields where you may feed on ambrosia, where no henbane groweth, but where sweet flowers cover the meads. And then you think you have some idea of heaven: and you sit down and say, "It is sweet to hear that man speak; he carried me so away; he made me think I was there; he gave me such conceptions as I never head before; he worked on my imagination." And do you know, there is not a greater power than imagination. I would not give a farthing for a man who has not imagination; he is of no use, if he wishes to move the multitude. If you were to take away my imagination I must die. It's a little heaven below, to imagine sweet things. But never think that imagination can picture heaven. When it is most sublime when it is freest from the dust of earth, when it is carried up by he greatest knowledge, and kept steady by the most extreme caution, imagination cannot picture heaven. "It hath not entered the heart of man, the things which God hath prepared for them that love him." Imagination is good, but not to picture to us heaven. Your imaginary heaven you will find by-and-by to be all a mistake; though you may have piled up fine castles, you will find them to be castles in the air, and they will vanish like thin clouds before the gale. For imagination cannot make a heaven. "Eye hath not seen, nor ear heard, neither hath it entered the heart of man to conceive" it.

Our next point is, that *it is not a heaven of the* INTELLECT. Men who take to themselves the title of intelligent, and who very humbly and modestly call themselves philosophers, generally describe heaven as a place where we shall know all things; and their grandest idea of heaven is, that they shall discover all secrets there. There the rock which would not tell its origin shall bubble forth its history; there the star which would not tell its date, and could not be made to whisper of its inhabitants, shall at once unravel all its secrets; there the animal, the fashion of which could scarcely be guessed at, so long had it been buried amongst other fossils in the earth, shall start up again, and it shall be seen of what form and shape it really was:—there the rocky secrets of this our earth that they never could discover will be opened to them; and they conceive that they shall travel from one star to another star, from planet to planet, and fill their enobled intellect, as they now delight to call it, with all kinds of human knowledge. They reckon that heaven will be to understand the works of the Creator: and concerning such men as Bacon and other great philosophers, of whose piety we generally have very little evidence, we read at the end of their biographies—"He has now departed, that noble spirit which taught us such glorious things here, to sip at the fountain of knowledge, and have all his mistakes rectified, and his doubts cleared up." But we do not believe anything of the kind. Intellect! thou knowest it now! "It hath not entered into the heart of man." It is high; what canst thou know? It is deep; what canst thou understand? It is only the Spirit that can give you a guess of heaven.

Now we come to the point—"He hath revealed it unto us by his Spirit." I think this means, that it was revealed unto the apostles by the Spirit, so that they wrote something of it in the Holy Word; but as you all believe that, we will only hint at it, and pass on. We think also that it refers to every believer, and that every believer does have glimpses of heaven below, and that God does reveal heaven to him, even whilst on earth, so that he understands what heaven is, in some measure. I love to talk of the Spirit's influence on man. I am a firm believer in the doctrine of impulse, in the doctrine of influence, in the doctrine of direction, in the doctrine of instruction by the Holy Spirit; and I believe him to be an interpreter, one of a thousand, who reveals unto man his own sinfulness, and afterwards teaches him his righteousness in Christ Jesus. I know there are some who abuse that doctrine, and ascribe every text that comes into their heart as given by the Spirit. We have heard of a man who, passing by his neighbour's wood, and having none in his own house, fancied he should like to take some. The text crossed his mind—"In all these things Job sinned not." He said, "There is an influence from the Spirit; I must take that man's wood." Presently, however, conscience whispered, "Thou shalt not steal;" and he remembered then that no text could have been put into his heart by the Spirit, if it excused sin or led him into it. However we do not discard the doctrine of impulse, because some people make a mistake; and we shall have a little of it this morning—a little of the teaching of God's gracious Spirit, whereby he reveals unto us what heaven is.

First of all, we think a Christian gets a gaze of what heaven is, *when in the midst of trials and troubles he is able to cast all his care upon the Lord,* because he careth for him. When waves of distress, and billows of affliction pass over the Christian, there are times when his faith is so strong that he lies down and sleeps, though the hurricane is thundering in his ears, and though billows are rocking him like a child in its cradle, though the earth is removed, and the mountains are carried into the midst of the sea, he says, "God is our refuge and strength, a very present help in trouble." Famine and desolation come; but he says, "Though the fig tree shall not blossom, neither shall there be fruit on the vine, though the labour of the olive shall fail, and the field shall yield no increase, yet will I trust in the Lord, and stay myself on the God of Jacob." Affliction smites him to the ground; he looks up, and says, "Though he slay me, yet will I trust in him." The blows that are given to him are like the lashing of a whip upon the water, covered up immediately, and he seems to feel nothing. It is not stoicism; it is the peculiar sleep of the beloved. "So he giveth his beloved sleep." Persecution surrounds him; but he is unmoved. Heaven is something like that—a place of holy calm and trust—

"That holy calm, that sweet repose,
Which none but he who feels it knows.
This heavenly calm within the breast
Is the dear pledge of glorious rest,
Which for the church of God remains,
The end of cares, the end of pains."

But there is another season in which the Christian has heaven revealed to him; and that is, *the season of quiet contemplation*. There are precious hours, blessed be God, when we forget the world—times and seasons when we get quite away from it, when our weary spirit wings its way far, far, from scenes of toil and strife. There are precious moments when the angel of contemplation gives us a vision. He comes and puts his finger on the lip of the noisy world; he bids the wheels that are continually rattling in our ears be still; and we sit down, and there is a solemn silence of the mind. We find our heaven and our God; we engage ourselves in contemplating the glories of Jesus, or mounting upwards towards the bliss of heaven—in going backward to the great secrets of electing love, in considering the immutability of the blessed covenant, in thinking of what wind which "bloweth where it listeth," in remembering our own participation of that life which cometh from God, in thinking of our blood-bought union with the Lamb, of the consummation of our marriage with him in realms of light and bliss, or any such kindred topics. Then it is that we know a little about heaven. Have ye never found, O ye sons and daughters of gaiety, a holy calm come over you at times, in reading the thoughts of your fellowmen? But oh! how blessed to come and read the thoughts of God, and work, and weave them out in contemplation. Then we have a web of contemplation that we wrap around us like an enchanted garment, and we open our eyes and see heaven. Christian! when you are enabled by the Spirit to hold a season of sweet contemplation, then you can say—"But he hath revealed them unto us by his Spirit;" for the joys of heaven are akin to the joys of contemplation, and the joys of a holy calm in God. But there are times with me—I dare say there may be with some of you—when we do something more than contemplate—when we arise by meditation above thought itself, and when our soul, after having touched the Pisgah of contemplation by the way, flies positively into the heavenly places in Christ Jesus. There are seasons when the Spirit not only stands and flaps his wings o'er the gulf, but positively crosses the Jordan and dwells with Christ, holds fellowship with angels, and talks with spirits—gets up there with Jesus, clasps him in his arms, and cries, "My beloved is mine, and I am his; I will hold him, and will not let him go." I know what it is at times to lay my beating head on the bosom of Christ with something more than faith— actually and positively to get hold of him; not only to take him by faith, but actually and positively to feed on him; to feel a vital union with him, to grasp his arm, and feel his very pulse beating. You say. "Tell it not to unbelievers; they will laugh!" Laugh ye may; but when we are there we care not for your laughter, if ye should laugh as loud as devils; for one moment's fellowship with Jesus would recompense us for it all. Picture not fairy lands; this is heaven, this is bliss. "He hath revealed it unto us by his Spirit."

And let not the Christian, who says he has very little of this enjoyment be discouraged. Do not think you cannot have heaven revealed to you by the Spirit; I tell you, you can, if you are one of the Lord's people. And let me tell some of you, that one of the places where you may most of all expect to see heaven is at the Lord's table. There are some of you, my dearly beloved, who absent yourselves from the supper of the Lord on earth; let me tell you in God's name, that you are not only sinning against God, but robbing yourselves of a most inestimable privilege. If there is one season in which the soul gets into closer communion with Christ than another, it is at the Lord's table. How often have we sang there,

"Can I Gethesemane forget?
Or there thy conflicts see,

59

Thine agony and bloody sweat,
And not remember thee?
Remember thee and all thy pains,
And all thy love to me,—
Yes, while a pulse, or breath remains,
I will remember thee."

And then you see what an easy transition it is to heaven:—

"And when these failing lips grow dumb,
And thought and memory flee;
When thou shalt in thy kingdom come,
Jesus, remember me."

O my erring brethren, ye who live on, unbaptized, and who receive not this sacred supper, I tell you not that they will save you—most assuredly they will not, and if you are not saved before you receive them they will be an injury to you;—but if you are the Lord's people, why need you stay away? I tell you, the Lord's table is so high a place that you can see heaven from it very often. You get so near the cross there, you breathe so near the cross, that your sight becomes clearer, and the air brighter, and you see more of heaven there than anywhere else. Christian, do not neglect the supper of thy Lord; for it thou dost, he will hide heaven from thee, in a measure.

Again, how sweetly do we realize heaven, *when we assemble in our meetings for prayer.* I do not know how my brethren feel at prayer meetings; but they are so much akin to what heaven is, as a place of devotion, that I really think we get more ideas of heaven by the Spirit there, than in hearing a sermon preached, because the sermon necessarily appeals somewhat to the intellect and the imagination. But if we enter into the vitality of prayer at our prayer meetings, then it is the Spirit that reveals heaven to us. I remember two texts that I preached from lately at our Monday evening meeting, which were very sweet to some of our souls. "Abide with us, for the day is far spent," and another, "By night on my bed I sought him whom my soul loveth: I sought him and found him." Then indeed we held some foretaste of heaven. Master Thomas would not believe that his Lord was risen. Why? Because he was not at the last prayer-meeting; for we are told that Thomas was not there. And those who are often away from devotional meetings are very apt to have doubting frames; they do not get sights of heaven, for they get their eye-sight spoiled by stopping away.

Another time when we get sights of heaven is in *extraordinary closet seasons*. Ordinary closet prayer will only make ordinary Christians of us. It is in extraordinary seasons, when we are led by God to devote, say an hour, to earnest prayer—when we feel an impulse, we scarce know why, to cut off a portion of our time during the day to go alone. Then, beloved, we kneel down, and begin to pray in earnest. It may be that we are attacked by the devil; for when the enemy knows we are going to have a great blessing, he always makes a great noise to drive us away; but if we keep at it, we shall soon get into a quiet frame of mind, and hear him roaring at a distance. Presently you get hold of the angel, and say, "Lord, I will not let thee go, except thou bless me." He asks your name. You begin to tell him what you name was:

> "Once a sinner, near despair,
> Sought thy mercy-seat by prayer;
> Mercy heard and set him free;
> Lord, that mercy came to me."

You say, "What is thy name, Lord?" He will not tell you. You hold him fast still; at last he deigns to bless you. That is certainly some foretaste of heaven, when you feel alone with Jesus. Let no man know your prayers; they are between God and yourselves; but if you want to know much of heaven, spend some extra time in prayer; for God then reveals it to us by his Spirit.

"Behold, ye despisers, and wonder, and perish." You have been saying in your hearts, "The prophet is a fool, and this spiritual man is mad." Go away and say these things; but be it known unto you, that what ye style madness is to us wisdom and what ye count folly "is the wisdom of God in a mystery, even the hidden wisdom." And if there is a poor penitent here this morning, saying, "Ah! sir, I get visions enough of hell, but I do not get visions of heaven;" poor penitent sinner, thou canst not have any visions of heaven, unless thou lookest through the hands of Christ. The only glass through which a poor sinner can see bliss is that formed by the holes in Jesus' hands. Dost thou not know, that all grace and mercy was put into the hand of Christ, and that it never could have run out to thee unless his hand had been bored through in crucifixion. He cannot hold it from thee, for it will run through; and he cannot hold it in his heart, for he has got a rent in it made by the spear. Go and confess your sin to him, and he will wash you, and make you whiter than snow. If you feel you cannot repent, go to him and tell him so, for he is exalted to give repentance, as well as remission of sins. Oh! that the spirit of God might give you true repentance and true faith; and then saint and sinner shall meet together, and both shall not only know what "eye hath not seen, nor ear heard;" but,

> "Then shall we see, and hear, and know
> All we desired or wished below,
> And every power find sweet employ
> In that eternal world of joy."

Till that time we can only have these things revealed to us by the Spirit; and we will seek more of that, each day we live.

5

The Heaven of Heaven

"And they shall see His face."

—Revelation 22:4

THE ITALIANS SO MUCH ADMIRE the city of Naples that their proverb is, "See Naples and die," as if there remained nothing more to be seen after that fair bay and city had been gazed upon. To behold the far fairer sight mentioned in the text, men might well be content to die a thousand times! If it shall please God that we shall depart this life before the Master's appearing, we may laugh at death, and count it to be *gain*, seeing that it introduces us to the place where we shall see His face. "You cannot see My face and live," said the Lord of old, but that was true of *mortals* only, and refers not to *immortals* who have put on incorruption! In yonder Glory they see the face of God, and yet live; yes, the sight is the essence and excellence of their life! Here, that vision might be too overpowering for the soul and body, and might painfully separate them with excess of delight, and so *cause* us death; but up yonder the disembodied spirit is able to endure the blaze of splendor, and so will the body, when it shall have been refined and strengthened in its powers by resurrection from the dead. Then these eyes, which now would be struck with blindness should they look upon the superlative Glory, shall be strengthened to behold eternally the Lord of Angels who is the brightness of His Father's Glory, and the express Image of His Person.

Brothers and Sisters, regard the object of our expectations! See the happiness which is promised us! Behold the Heaven which awaits us! Forget, for a while, your present cares; let all your difficulties and your sorrows vanish for a season, and live for a while in the future which is so certified by faithful Promises that you may rejoice in it even *now!* The veil which parts us from our great reward is very thin; Hope gazes through its gauzy fabric; Faith, with eagle eyes, penetrates the mist which hides eternal delights from longing eyes. "Eye has not seen, nor ear heard, neither have entered into the heart of man the things which God has prepared for them who love Him; but He has revealed them unto us by His Spirit, for the Spirit searches all things, even the deep things of God." And we, in the Power of that Spirit, have known, believed, and anticipated the bliss which every winged hour is bringing nearer to us. While our Lord was here below, it would have been a great delight to spiritual minds to have seen His face; I can scarcely imagine, but perhaps some of you mothers can, what must have been the joy that flooded the heart of Mary when, for the first time, she gazed upon the lovely face of the Holy Child Jesus.

I suppose the Infant Jesus to have possessed an extraordinary beauty; a soul absolutely perfect as His was, must surely have been enshrined in a body perfect in its symmetry, and attractive in its features. The overshadowing Spirit, by whose miraculous agency He was conceived of the Virgin, would scarcely have created an uncomely body, and much less would He have fashioned an unlovely body for so delightful a Person as the Only-Begotten of the Father! I think as His virgin mother looked upon Him, and as the wise men, and the shepherds gazed into that dear face, they might all have said with the spouse of old, "You are fairer than the children of men." That manger held an unrivalled form of beauty! Well may painters strain their art to paint the mother, and her wondrous Child, for the spectacle brought shepherds from their flocks, sages from the far-off land, and angels from their thrones—Heaven and earth were alike intent to see His face! It would have been no small joy, I think, to have seen the face of Jesus of Nazareth in the years of His maturity, when His Countenance beamed with joy. "At that hour Jesus rejoiced in spirit, and said, Father, I thank You." One would like to have basked in the radiance of a *sinless* smile—it was a vision fit only for the pure in heart to have traced the fair marks of joy upon the face of Jesus, and such a joy, so spiritual, so refined, so heavenly, so Divine! "Father, I thank You," blessing God for that Eternal Decree of Election by which He has hidden the things of the Kingdom from the wise and prudent, and has revealed them unto babes, and saying, "Even so, Father, for so it seemed good in Your sight."

Equally rare must have been the vision which Peter, and James, and John beheld when they looked into that Savior's face, and saw it Transfigured—beams of light flashing from its every feature, and His whole Person made to glow with a superhuman splendor! The favored spectator might well be content to die at that moment! It was enough to have lived to have beheld His Glory so Divinely revealed! Beloved, have you not sometimes felt as I have, that you could have wished to have seen the Well-Beloved's face even in its grief and agony? It was not long before the beauty of Jesus began to be marred by His inward griefs and His daily hardships; He appears to have looked like a man of 50 when He was scarcely thirty. The Jews said, "You are not yet 50 years old, and have You seen Abraham?" His visage was more marred, we are told, than that of any man, and His form more than the sons of men, for He took upon Himself our sickness, and bore our sorrows; and all this substitutionary grief plowed deep furrows upon that blessed brow, and made the cheeks to sink, and the eyes to become red with much weeping. Yet gladly would I have gazed into the face of the Man of Sorrows! Gladly would I have seen those eyes which were "as the eyes of doves by the rivers of waters, washed with milk and fitly set." Gladly would I have seen those founts of pity, wells of love, and springs of grief! Gladly would I have adoringly admired those cheeks which were as beds of spices, as sweet flowers, and those lips like lilies dropping sweet-smelling myrrh. All the suffering that He suffered could not take away from that marred visage its majesty of Grace and Holiness, nor withdraw from it one whit of that mental, moral, and spiritual beauty which were peculiar to the perfect Man. O how terribly lovely that beloved face must have looked when it was covered with the crimson of the bloody sweat, when the radiant hues of His rosy sufferings suffused the lily of His perfection!

What a vision must that have been of the Man of Sorrows when He said, "My soul is exceedingly sorrowful, even unto death"; what must it have been to have looked into His face when His brow was girt about with the crown of thorns; when the ruby drops followed each other adown those bruised cheeks which had been spit upon by the shameful mouths of the scorners. That must have been a spectacle of woe, indeed, but perhaps, yet more ghastly still, was the face of the Redeemer when He said, "I thirst!" Or when, in bitterest anguish, He shrieked, "My God, My God, why have You forsaken Me?" Then, indeed, the sun of the universe suffered a horrible eclipse! Then the light of Heaven, for a while, passed under a black tempestuous cloud! That face in such a condition we have not seen, nor shall see, but Beloved, we *shall see His face*. I could have wished to have been with Mary, and the holy women, and Joseph, and Nicodemus when they took His blessed body from the Cross, and laid it in the tomb. O for one gaze into that poor pale dead face—to have seen how death looked when mirrored in that matchless clay! And to see how Jesus appeared when conquered, and yet *conquering;* vanquished and yet the Victor; yielding up His body to the spoiler to be laid, for a while, in the treasure house of the tomb, and yet bursting all the bars of the spoiler's den!

But, Brothers and Sisters, there was a glorious change, no doubt, in the face of our Lord when it was seen by several brethren after the Resurrection. It was the same face, and they knew Him to be the same Christ. Did they not put their fingers into the nail prints, and thrust their hand into

65

His side? Did they not know Him to be veritable flesh and bone as they saw Him eat the piece of fish and honeycomb? But the face was restored to its former majesty and radiance, for I suppose it to have beamed with the dawn; flashes of that light which now flames forth from it, of which John says, "His face was as the sun shining in its strength." There were, we believe, some soft unveilings of that unexampled Glory which glorified saints, day without night, are perpetually beholding in Heaven. That face was for the last time seen when He Ascended, and the clouds concealed Him; then, gazing downward, and scattering benedictions with both His hands, He appointed His disciples to be His witnesses, and bade them go and preach His Gospel, for He would be with them always, even unto the end of the world. Such was the face of Christ on earth—and the remembrance may serve to inspire in us a holy panting after the Beatific Vision which the Lord has promised us, and of which we are now about to speak as the Holy Spirit may graciously give us utterance.

First, this morning I purpose, Brothers and Sisters, to bring before your minds the Beatific Vision itself—*"They shall see His face";* then secondly, we shall dwell for a moment, upon the surpassing clearness of the vision: "They shall *see* His face"—in a sense more than usually emphatic; then thirdly, upon *the privileges, choice and precious, which are involved in the vision;* and lastly we shall have a word or two upon those favored ones who shall enjoy the sight— *"They,"* and none other—*"They shall see His face."*

I. First, then, THE BEATIFIC VISION. "They shall see His face." It is the chief blessing of Heaven, the cream of Heaven, the Heaven of Heaven, that the saints shall there see Jesus! There will be other things to see. Who dares despise those foundations of chrysolite, and chrysoprasus, and jacinth? Who shall speak lightly of streets of glassy gold, and gates of pearl? We would not forget that we shall see angels, and seraphim, and cherubim; nor would we fail to remember that we shall see Apostles, martyrs, and confessors together with those whom we have walked with, and communed with in our Lord while here below. We shall assuredly behold those of our departed kindred who sleep in Jesus, dear to us here, and dear to us still— "not lost, but gone before." But still, for all this, the main thought which we now have of Heaven, and certainly the main fullness of it when we shall be there, is just this—we shall see Jesus! We shall care little for any of those imaginary occupations which have such charms for a certain class of minds, that they could even find a Heaven in them; I have read fanciful periods in which the writer has found celestial joys to consist in an eternal progress in the knowledge of the laws of God's universe. Such is not *my* Heaven!

66

Knowledge is not happiness, but on the contrary, is often an increase of sorrow; knowing of itself, does not make men happy nor holy; for mere knowing's sake, I would as soon not know as know, if I had my choice—better to love an ounce than to know a pound! Better a little service than much knowledge! I desire to know what God pleases to teach me, but beyond that, even ignorance shall be my bliss!

Some have talked of flitting from star to star, seeing the wonders of God throughout the universe; how He rules in this province of His wide domain; how He governs in that other region of His vast dominion. It may be so, but it would be no Heaven to me! So far as I can at present judge, I would rather stay at home, and sit at the feet of Christ forever than roam over the wide creation—

> "The spacious earth and spreading flood
> Proclaim the wise and powerful God,
> And Your rich glories from afar
> Sparkle in every rolling star.
> Yet in Christ's looks a Glory stands,
> The noblest wonder of God's hands;
> He, in the Person of His Son,
> Has all His mightiest works outdone."

If Jesus were not Infinite, we should not speak so, but since He is, in His Person Divine, and as to His Manhood so nearly allied to us that the closest possible sympathy exists between us, there will always be fresh subjects for thought, fresh sources for enjoyment for those who are taken up with Him. Certainly, Brothers and Sisters, to no Believer would Heaven be desirable if Jesus were not there, or, if being there, they could not enjoy the nearest and dearest fellowship with Him. A sight of Him first turned our sorrow into joy; renewed communion with Him lifts us above our present cares, and strengthens us to bear our heavy burdens. What must *heavenly* communion be? When we have Christ with us, we are content with a crumb, and satisfied with a cup of water, but if His face is hidden, the whole world cannot afford a solace—we are widowed of our Beloved, our sun has set, our moon is eclipsed, and our candle is blown out!

Christ is All in All to us here, and therefore we pant and long for a Heaven in which He shall be All in All to us forever—and such *will* the Heaven of God be! The Paradise of God is not the Elysium of imagination, the Utopia of intellect, or the Eden of poetry—it is the Heaven of intense *spiritual* fellowship with the Lord Jesus, a place where it is promised to faithful souls that "they shall see His face." In the Beatific Vision it is Christ whom they see! And further, it is His face which they behold; they shall not see the hem of His robe as Moses saw the back parts of Jehovah; they shall not be satisfied to touch the hem of His garment, or to sit far down at His feet where they can only see His sandals—no, they "shall see His face!" By this I understand two things; first, that they shall literally and physically, with their risen bodies, actually look into the face of Jesus; and secondly, that *spiritually* their mental faculties shall be enlarged so that they shall be enabled to look into the very heart, and soul, and Character of Christ, so as to understand Him, His work, His Love, as they never understood Him before. They shall literally, I say, see His face, for Christ is no phantom!

And in Heaven, though Divine, and therefore *spiritual*, He is still a Man, and therefore *material* like ourselves. The very flesh and blood that suffered upon Calvary is in Heaven! The hand that was pierced with the nail, now at this moment grasps the scepter of all worlds! That very head which was bowed down with anguish, is now crowned with a royal diadem, and the face that was no marvel is the very face which beams resplendent amidst the thrones of Heaven! Into that same Countenance we shall be permitted to gaze. O what a sight! Roll by years! Hasten on you laggard months and days, to let us but for once behold Him—our Beloved, our hearts' care, who "redeemed us unto God by His blood." Whose we are, and whom we love with such a passionate desire, that to be in His embrace we would be satisfied to suffer 10,000 deaths. *We shall actually see Jesus!*

Yet the *spiritual* sight will be sweeter still; I think the text implies that in the next world our powers of mind will be very different from what they are now. We are, the best of us in our infancy as yet, and know but in part, but we shall be men then—we shall "put away childish things." We shall see and know even as we are known, and among the great things that we shall know will be this greatest of all—that we shall know Christ! We shall know the heights, and depths, and lengths, and breadths of the Love of Christ that passes knowledge! O how delightful it will be then, to understand His Everlasting Love! How, without beginning, or ever the earth was, His thoughts darted forward towards His dear ones whom He had chosen in the Sovereignty of His choice, that they should be His forever; what a subject for delightful meditation will the Covenant be, and Christ's surety engagements in that Covenant when He undertook to take the debts of all His people upon Himself, and to pay them all, and to stand and suffer in their place. And what thoughts shall we have then of our union with Christ—our federal, vital, conjugal oneness! We only *talk* about these things now, we do not really *understand* them; we merely plow the surface, and gather a topsoil harvest, but a richer subsoil lies beneath. Brothers and Sisters, in Heaven we shall dive into the deepest depths of fellowship with Jesus; "We shall see His face," that is, we shall see clearly and plainly all that has to do with our Lord—and this shall be the topmost bliss of Heaven. In the blessed Vision the saints see Jesus, and they see Him clearly.

We may also remark that they see Him *always*, for when the text says, "They shall see His face," it implies that they never, at any time are without the sight. Never for a moment do they unlock their arm from the arm of their Beloved! They are not as we are—sometimes near the Throne, and then afar off by backslidings; sometimes hot with love, and then cold with indifference; they are not as we are, sometimes bright as seraphs, and then dull as clods, but forever and ever they are in closest association with the Master, for "they shall see His face." Best of all, they see His face as it is now in all its Glory. John tells us what that will be like. In his first Chapter he says, "His head and His hair were white like wool, as white as snow," to mark His Antiquity, for He is the Ancient of Days. "And His eyes were as a flame of fire; and His Countenance was as the sun shines in his strength." Such is the Vision which the Redeemed enjoy before the Throne! Their Lord is all brightness, and in Him there is nothing to weep over, nothing to mar His Glory! Doubtless there are traces there, upon that wondrous face, of all the griefs He once endured, but these only make Him more glorious; He looks like a lamb that has been slain, and still wears His priesthood; but all that has to do with the shame, and the spit, and slaughter, has been so transformed that the sight is all blissful, all comforting, all glorious! In His face there is nothing to excite a tear, or to beget a sigh.

I wish my lips were unloosed, and my thoughts were free, that I could tell you something more of this sight, but indeed, it is not given unto mortal tongues to talk of these things. I suppose that if we were caught up to see His face, and should come back again, yet would we have to say like Paul, that we had heard and seen that which it was not lawful for us to utter. God will not as yet reveal these things fully to us, but He reserves His best wine for the last; we can but give you a few glimpses, but O Beloved, wait a little while—it shall not be long before you shall see His face!

II. Secondly, we turn to another thought—THE SURPASSING CLEARNESS OF THAT VISION. "They shall see His face." The word, "see" sounds in my ears with a clear, full, melodious note. I think we see but little here. This indeed, is not the world of sight—"we walk by faith, not by

69

sight." Around us all is mist and cloud; what we *do* see, we see only as if men were trees walking. If ever we get a glimpse of the spirit-world, it is like yonder momentary lightning flash in the darkness of the tempest which opens for an instant the gates of Heaven, and in the twinkling of an eye they are closed again. And then the darkness is denser than before, as if it were enough for us poor mortals to know that there is a brightness denied to us as yet. The saints see the face of Jesus in Heaven because they are purified from sin. The pure in heart are blessed, they shall see God, and none others. It is because of our impurity which still remains, that we cannot as yet see His face, but *their* eyes are touched with eye salve, and therefore they see. Ah, Brothers and Sisters, how often does our Lord Jesus hide Himself behind the clouds of dust which we ourselves make by our unholy walking! If we become proud, or selfish, or slothful, or fall into any other of our besetting sins, then our eyes lose their capacity to behold the brightness of our Lord.

But up yonder they not only do not sin, but they *cannot* sin; they are not tempted, for there is no space for the Tempter to work upon, even could he be admitted to try them. They are without fault before the Throne of God, and surely this alone is a Heaven—to be rid of inbred sin, and the plague of the heart, and to have ended forever, the struggle of spiritual life, the crushing of the fleshly power of death! They may well see His face when the scales of sin have been taken from their eyes, and they have become pure as God Himself is pure! They surely see His face more clearly, because all the clouds of care are gone from them. Some of you, while sitting here today, have been trying to lift up your minds to heavenly contemplation, but you cannot; the business has gone so wrong this week; the children have vexed you so much; sickness has been in the house so sorely; you feel in your body you are quite out of order for devotion—these enemies break your concentration. Now *they* are vexed by none of these things in Heaven, and therefore they can see their Master's face! They are not cumbered with Martha's cares; they still occupy Mary's seat at His feet. When you and I have laid aside the farm, and the merchandise, and the marrying, and the burying which come so fast upon each other's heels, we shall then, be forever with the Lord—

> "Far from a world of grief and sin,
> With God eternally shut in"!

Moreover, as they have done with sins and cares, so have they done with sorrows. "There shall be no more death, neither sorrow, nor crying; neither shall there be any more pain, for the former things are passed away."

We are none of us quite strangers to grief, and with some of us pain is an inseparable companion—we still dwell in the smoky tents of Kedar. Perhaps it is well that we should be so tried while we are here, for sanctified sorrow refines the soul, but in Glory there is no affliction, for pure gold needs not the furnace. Well may they then, behold Christ when there are no tears to dim their eyes, no smoke of this world to rise up between them and their Beloved—they are alike, free from sin, and care, and sorrow! They see His face right gloriously in that cloudless atmosphere, and in the Light which He Himself supplies. Moreover, the glorified see His face the more clearly because there are no idols to stand between Him and them. Our idolatrous love of worldly things is a chief cause of our knowing so The Heaven of little of spiritual things; because we love this and that so much, we see little of Christ. You cannot fill your life cup from the pools of earth, and yet have room in it for the crystal streams of Heaven; but they have no idols there—nothing to occupy the heart, no rival for the Lord Jesus. He reigns supreme within their spirits, and therefore they see His face; they have no veils of ignorance or prejudice to darken their sight in Heaven.

Those of us who most candidly endeavor to learn the Truth of God, are nevertheless in some degree biased and warped by education. Let us struggle as we may, yet still our surroundings will not permit us to see things as they are. There is a deflection in our vision, a refraction in the air, a something everywhere which casts the beam of light out of its straight line, so that we see the *appearance* rather than the *reality* of the Truth of God. We see not with open sight; our vision is marred. But up yonder, among the golden harps, they "know, even as they are known." They have no prejudices, but a full desire to know the Truth—the bias is gone, and therefore they are able to see His face. O blessed thought! One could almost wish to sit down and say no more, but just roll that sweet morsel under one's tongue, and extract the essence and sweetness of it! "They see His face." There is no long distance for the eye to travel over, for they are near Him, they are in His bosom, they are sitting on His Throne at His right hand. No withdrawals there to mourn over—their sun shall no more go down! Here He stands behind our wall; He shows Himself through the lattices, but He hides not Himself in Heaven! O when shall the long summer days of Glory be ours, and Jesus our undying Joy forever and ever?

In Heaven they never pray—

"Oh may no earth-born cloud arise
To hide You from Your servant's eyes,"

but forever and forever they bask in the sunlight, or rather, like Milton's angel, they live in the Sun itself! They come not to the sea's brink to wade into it up to their ankles, but they swim in bliss forever! In waves of everlasting rest, in richest, closest fellowship with Jesus, they display themselves with ineffable delight!

III. The third part of the subject which commands our attention this morning is THE MATCHLESS PRIVILEGE WHICH THIS VISION INVOLVES. We may understand the words, *"they shall see His face,"* to contain five things. They mean, first, certain Salvation. The face of Jesus Christ acts in two ways upon the sons of men; with some it is a face of terror—"Before His face Heaven and earth fled away." It is written concerning Him, "Who may abide the day of His coming? And who shall stand when He appears? For He is like a refiner's fire, and like fullers' soap." A sight of Christ's face will be, to the *ungodly*, eternal absence from the Presence of the Lord! But if there are some men who shall see His face, who shall sit down, and delight themselves in gazing upon the face of the great Judge upon the Throne, then those persons are assuredly saved! They are awaiting the day of His coming; they are dwelling with the eternal flame without being consumed; they are resting on the bosom of our God who is a consuming fire; and yet, like the burning bush of old, though glowing with the Glory, they are not consumed by the heat. O happy men who can live where others must expire—who can find their Heaven where a carnal world must eternally find its Hell! This is the first thing in the text. "They shall see His face"—*then they are everlastingly safe.*

The second privilege is they shall have a clear *knowledge of Him.* I have dwelt upon that thought before, and merely mention it to complete the summary. To look into the face of Christ signifies to be well acquainted with His Person, His office, His Character, His work. So the saints in Heaven shall have more knowledge of Christ than the most advanced below. As one has said, the babe in Christ admitted to Heaven discovers more of Christ in a single hour than is known by all the divines of the assemblies of the Church on earth. O yes, our Catechisms and our creeds, and even our Bible—all these reveal but very little of what we shall discover when we shall see His face! Our text also implies *conscious favor.* Was not that the old benediction, "The Lord lift up His Countenance upon you"? He *has* lifted it up upon the *Glorified,* and they see it world without end! Here it is our joy of joys to have the Lord smiling upon us, for if He is with us, who can be against us? If we know that He loves us, and that He delights in us, it matters not to us though earth and Hell should hate us, and men cast out our names as evil. In Heaven then, they have this to be their choice privilege; they are courtiers who stand always in the Monarch's palace, secure of the Monarch's smile; they are children who live unbrokenly in their Father's Love, and know it, and rejoice to know it evermore!

The fourth privilege involved in the text is that of *close fellowship*. They are always near to Jesus; they are never *hoping* that they are with Him, and yet fearing that they are not; they have none of those inward struggles which make life so unhappy for some of us; they never say—"'Tis a point I long to know." They see His face, and are in hourly communion with their Lord. Perfect spirits are always walking with the Lord, for they are always agreed with Him. In Glory they are all Enochs, walking with God. There, forever and forever they lie in the bosom of Jesus, in the nearest possible place of communion with Him who redeemed them with His blood. And this involves a fifth privilege, namely, *complete transformation*. "They shall be like He, for they shall see Him as He is." If they see His face, they shall be "changed from glory to glory" by this face to face vision of the Lord. Beholding Christ, His likeness is photographed upon them—they become in all respects like He as they gaze upon Him world without end!

Thus have I very briefly mentioned the privileges involved in seeing Christ face to face.

IV. We must conclude by noting WHO THEY ARE TO WHOM THIS CHOICE GIFT IS AFFORDED BY DIVINE MERCY. "They shall see His face." Who are *they?* They are all His Elect, all His Redeemed, all His Effectually Called, all the Justified, all the Sanctified. They are the tens of thousands, and myriads who have died in Jesus, of whom the Spirit says, "Blessed are the dead which die in the Lord." Thank God we are not strangers to those who now behold His face! As we look back to the associations of our youth, and to the friendships of our manhood, we remember many whose privilege it has been to precede us, and to know long before us the things which we desire, and expect so soon to learn. Some are taken away to see His face while yet young; we bless God that our babes shall have the same Heaven as our holy parents—they shall not be placed in the back settlements of Canaan, but they shall with equal clearness, see the face of Jesus! Those dear boys and girls who learned to love Christ, and made a profession of His name in their youth; who were never spared to reach the ripeness of manhood and womanhood, they shall equally see His face with the gravest and most reverend fathers of the Church! I read of no secondary joys. Whoever may have invented the doctrine of degrees in Heaven I do not know, but I believe there is as much foundation for it in Scripture as there is for the doctrine of "purgatory," and no more! All the saints shall see their Master's face; the thief dying on the cross was with Christ in Paradise, and Paul could be no more!

I sometimes like to think of Heaven in the same way as old Ryland did when he wrote his rhyming letter from Northampton—

> "They all shall be there,
> The great and the small:
> For I shall shake hands
> With the blessed St. Paul."

Doubtless we all shall; whether dying young or old, whether departing after long service to Christ, or dying immediately after conversion as the thief, of all the saints shall it be said in the words of the text, "They shall see His face." What more can Apostles and martyrs enjoy? Do you regret that your friends have departed? Do you lament that wife, and husband, and child, and father, and grandparents have all entered into their rest? Be not so unkind, so selfish to yourself, so cruel to them! No, rather, soldier of the Cross, be thankful that another has won the crown before you, and you press forward to win it, too. Life is but a moment—how short it will appear in Eternity! Even here Hope perceives it to be brief, and though Impatience counts it long, yet Faith corrects her, and reminds her that one hour with God will make the longest life to seem but a point of time, a mere *nothing*, a watch in the night, a thing that was, and was not, that has come and gone!

So we will close our sermon by observing that they who see His face already make only a part of the great "they" who shall see His face—for many of us here below are on the way to the same reward! As many as have felt the burden of sin, and have come to the foot of the Cross, and looked to those five crimson founts—the wounds of Jesus; as many as can say, "He is all my salvation, and all my desire"; as many as can serve Him feeling that for them to live is Christ; as many as shall fight, day by day, against sin, and shall overcome through the blood of the Lamb; as many as by the Eternal Spirit's Power, shall be kept by faith unto Salvation—they shall all see His face! It is mine to hope to see it, and it is yours, too, Beloved, and the hope shall not be disappointed! It makes not ashamed! We shall see His face, and that vision shall yield us perfect bliss!

Yet I fear my text is not true of all here assembled. Just this word for the unconverted—I am afraid you may almost say with Balaam, "I shall see Him but not now; I shall behold Him, but not near," for every eye *shall* see

Him, and they, also, which crucified Him—and what will *they* say when they see Him? These ungodly ones—what will *they* do? They shall cry to the rocks, "Hide us!" And to the mountains, "Cover us from the face of Him who sits on the Throne." Ah, my dear Hearer, what a dreadful thing it will be if that very face which is the Heaven of your mother, and the Heaven of your husband, or the Heaven of your wife, and of your child, should be the Hell to *you* from which you shall desire to be *hidden!* Now it will be the case unless first of all, you seek His face on earth. Certain Greeks said to the disciples, "Sir, we would see Jesus." I wish *you* had that same desire this morning in a *spiritual* sense, for He Himself has said, "Look unto Me, and be you saved, all the ends of the earth." If you see Him now by simple faith, as your Savior, you shall see Him at the last as your King, your Friend, your Beloved! But you must first see Him to trust Him *here*, or you shall not see Him to rejoice in Him hereafter—

> "You sinners, seek His face,
> Whose wrath you cannot bear!
> Fly to the shelter of His Cross,
> And find Salvation there."

May God, even our own God, bless you for Jesus' sake. Amen.

6
Heavenly Worship

"And I looked, and, lo, a Lamb stood on the Mount Sion, and with him an hundred forty and four thousand, having his Father's name written in their foreheads. And I heard a voice from heaven, as the voice of many waters, and as the voice of a great thunder: and I heard the voice of harpers harping with their harps; And they sung as it were a new song before the throne, and before the four beasts, and the elders; and no man could learn that song but the hundred and forty and four thousand, which were redeemed from the earth."

—Revelation 14:1-3

THE SCENE OF THIS MARVELLOUS and magnificent vision is laid upon Mount Sion; by which we are to understand, not Mount Sion upon earth, but Mount Sion which is above, "Jerusalem, the mother of us all." To the Hebrew mind Mount Sion was a type of heaven, and very justly so. Among all the mountains of the earth none was to be found so famous as Sion. It was there that patriarch Abraham drew his knife to slay his son; it was there, too, in commemoration of that great triumph of faith, Solomon built a majestic temple, "beautiful for situation and the joy of the whole earth." That Mount Sion was the centre of all the devotions of the Jews.

"Up to her courts, with joys unknown,
The sacred tribes repaired."

Between the wings of the cherubim Jehovah dwelt; on the one altar there all the sacrifices were offered to high heaven. They loved Mount Sion, and often did they sing, when they drew nigh to her, in their annual pilgrimages, "How amiable are thy tabernacles O Lord God of hosts, my King and my God!" Sion is now desolate; she hath been ravished by the enemy; she hath been utterly destroyed; her vail hath been rent asunder, and the virgin daughter of Sion is now sitting in sackcloth and ashes; but, nevertheless, to the Jewish mind it must ever, in its ancient state, remain the best and sweetest type of heaven. John, therefore, when he saw this sight might have said, "I looked, and, lo, a Lamb stood in heaven, and with him an hundred and forty and four thousand having his Father's name written in their foreheads: And I heard a voice from heaven, as the voice of many waters, and as the voice of a great thunder; and I heard the voice of harpers harping with their harps: And they sung as it were a new song before the throne, and before the four beasts, and the elders: and no man could learn that song but the hundred and forty and four thousand, which were redeemed from the earth."

This morning I shall endeavour to show you, first of all, *the object of heavenly worship*—the Lamb in the midst of the throne; in the next place we shall look at *the worshippers themselves*, and note their manner and their character; in the third place we shall listen *to hear their song*, for we may almost hear it; it is like "the noise of many waters and like great thunder;" and then we shall close by noting, that it is *a new song* which they sing, and by endeavouring to mention one or two reasons why it must necessarily be so.

I. In the first place, then, we wish to take a view of THE OBJECT OF HEAVENLY WORSHIP. The divine John was privileged to look within the gates of pearl; and on turning round to tell us what he saw—observe how he begins—he saith not, "I saw streets of gold or walls of Jasper;" he saith not, "I saw crowns, marked their lustre, and saw the wearers." That he shall notice afterwards. But he begins by saying, "I looked, and, lo, a Lamb!" To teach us that the very first and chief object of attraction in the heavenly state is "the Lamb of God which taketh away the sins of the world." Nothing else attracted the Apostle's attention so much as the person of that Divine Being, who is the Lord God, our most blessed Redeemer: "I looked, and, lo a Lamb!" Beloved, if we were allowed to look within the vail which parts us from the world of spirits, we should see, first of all, the person of our Lord Jesus. If now we could go where the immortal spirits "day without night circle the throne rejoicing," we should see each of them with their faces turned in one direction; and if we should step up to one of the blessed spirits, and say, "O bright immortal, why are thine eyes fixed? What is it that absorbs thee quite, and wraps thee up in vision?" He, without deigning to give an answer, would simply point to the centre of the sacred circle, and lo, we should see a Lamb in the midst of the throne. They have not yet ceased to admire his beauty, and marvel at his wonders and adore his person.

> "Amidst a thousand harps and songs,
> Jesus, our God, exalted reigns."

He is the theme of song and the subject of observation of all the glorified spirits and of all the angels in paradise. "I looked, and, lo, a Lamb!"

Christian, here is joy for thee; thou hast looked, and thou hast seen the Lamb. Through thy tearful eyes thou hast seen the Lamb taking away thy sins. Rejoice, then! In a little while, when thine eyes shall have been wiped from tears, thou wilt see the same Lamb exalted on his throne. It is the joy of the heart to hold daily fellowship and communion with Jesus; thou shalt have the same joy in heaven; "there shalt thou see him as he is, and thou shalt be like him." Thou shalt enjoy the constant vision of his presence, and thou shalt dwell with him for aye. "I looked, and, lo, a Lamb!" Why, that Lamb is heaven itself; for as good Rutherford says, "Heaven and Christ are the same things; to be with Christ is to be in heaven, and to be in heaven is to be with Christ." And he very sweetly says in one of his letters, wrapped up in love to Christ. "Oh! my Lord Christ, if I could be in heaven without thee, it would be a hell; and if I could be in hell, and have thee still, it would be a heaven to me, for thou art all the heaven I want." It is true, is it not Christian? Does not thy soul say so?

> "Not all the harps above
> Could make a heavenly place,
> Should Christ his residence remove,
> Or but conceal his face."

All thou needest to make thee blessed, supremely blessed, is "to be with Christ, which is far better."

And now observe *the figure under which Christ is represented in heaven.* "I looked, and, lo, a Lamb." Now, you know Jesus, in Scripture, is often represented as a lion: he is so to his enemies, for he devoureth them, and teareth them to pieces. "Beware, ye that forget God, lest he tear *you* in pieces, and there be none to deliver." But in heaven he is in the midst of his friends, and therefore he,

> Looks like a lamb that has been slain,
> And wears his priesthood still."

Why should Christ in heaven choose to appear under the figure of a lamb, and not in some other of his glorious characters? We reply, because it was as a lamb that Jesus fought and conquered, and, therefore as a lamb he appears in heaven. I have read of certain military commanders, when they were conquerors, that on the anniversary of their victory they would never wear anything but the garment in which they fought. On that memorable day they say, "Nay, take away the robes; I will wear the garment which has been embroidered with the sabre-cut, and garnished with the shot that hath riddled it; I will wear no other garb but that in which I fought and conquered." It seems as if the same feeling possessed the breast of Christ. "As a Lamb," saith he, "I died, and worsted hell; as a Lamb I have redeemed my people, and therefore as a Lamb I will appear in paradise."

But, perhaps, there is another reason; it is to encourage us to come to him in prayer. Ah, believer, we need not be afraid to come to Christ, for he is a Lamb. To a lion-Christ we need fear to come; but the Lamb-Christ!—oh, little children, were ye ever afraid of lambs? Oh, children of the living God, should ye ever fail to tell your griefs and sorrows into the breast of one who is a Lamb? Ah, let us come boldly to the throne of the heavenly grace, seeing a Lamb sits upon it. One of the things which tend very much to spoil prayer-meetings is the fact that our brethren do not pray boldly. They would practice reverence, as truly they ought, but they should remember that the highest reverence is consistent with true familiarity. No man more reverent than Luther; no man more fully carried out for the passage, "He talked with his Maker as a man talketh with his friend." We may be as reverent as the angels, and yet we may be as familiar as children in Christ Jesus. Now, our friends, when they pray, very frequently say the same thing every time. They are Dissenters; they cannot bear the Prayer Book; they think that forms of prayer are bad, but they always use their own form of prayer notwithstanding; as much as if they were to say that the bishop's form would not do, but their own they must always use. But a form of prayer being wrong, is as much wrong when I make it as when the bishop makes it; I am as much out of order in using what I compose myself continually and constantly, as I am when I am using one that has been composed for me; perhaps far more so, as it is not likely to be one-half so good. If our friends, however, would lay aside the form into which they grow, and break up the stereotyped plates with which they print their prayers so often, they might come boldly to the throne of God, and need never fear to do so; for he whom they address is represented in heaven under the figure of a Lamb, to teach us to come close to him, and tell him all our wants, believing that he will not disdain to hear them.

And you will further notice that *this Lamb is said to stand.* Standing is the posture of triumph. The Father said to Christ, "Sit thou on my throne, till I make thine enemies thy footstool." It is done; they are his footstool, and here he is said to stand erect, like a victor over all his enemies. Many a time the Saviour knelt in prayer; once he hung upon the cross; but when the great scene of our text shall be fully wrought out, he shall stand erect, as more than conqueror, through his own majestic might. "I looked, and, lo, a Lamb stood on the Mount Sion." Oh, if we could rend the veil—if now we were privileged to see within it—there is no sight would so enthrall us as the simple sight of the Lamb in the midst of the throne. My dear brethren and sisters in Christ Jesus, would it not be all the sight you would ever wish to see, if you could once behold him whom your soul loveth? Would it not be a heaven to you, if it were carried out in your experience—"Mine eye shall see him, and not another's?" Would you want anything else to make you happy but continually to see him? Can you not say with the poet—

"Millions of years my wondering eyes
Shall o'er my Saviour's beauty rove,
And endless ages I'll adore
The wonders of his love?"

And if a single glimpse of him on earth affords you profound delight; it must be, indeed, a very sea of bliss, and an abyss of paradise, without a bottom or a shore, to see him as he is; to be lost in his splendours, as the stars are lost in the sunlight, and to hold fellowship with him, as did John the beloved, when he leaned his head upon his bosom. And this shall be thy lot, to see the Lamb in the midst of the throne.

II. The second point is, THE WORSHIPPERS, WHO ARE THEY? Turn to the text, and you will not, first of all, *their numbers*—"I looked, and, lo, a Lamb stood on the Mount Sion, and with him an hundred forty and four thousand." This is a certain number put for an uncertain—I mean uncertain to us, though not uncertain to God. It is a vast number, put for that "multitude which no man can number," who shall stand before the throne of God. Now, here is something not very pleasant to my friend Bigot yonder. Note the number of those who are to be saved; they are said to be a great number, even a "hundred forty and four thousand," which is but a unit put for the vast innumerable multitude who are to be gathered home. Why, my friend, there are so many as that belonging to your church. You believe that none will be saved but those who hear your minister, and believe your creed; I do not think you could find one hundred and forty-four thousand anywhere. You will have to enlarge your heart I think; you must take in a few more, and not be so inclined to shut out the Lord's people, because you cannot agree with them. I do abhor from my heart that continual whining of some men about their own little church as the "remnant"—the "few that are to be saved." They are always dwelling upon strait gates and narrow ways, and upon what they conceive to be a truth, that but few shall enter heaven. Why, my friends, I believe there will be more in heaven than in hell. If you ask me why I think so, I answer, because Christ, in everything, is to "have the pre-eminence," and I cannot conceive how he could have the pre-eminence if there are to be more in the dominions of Satan than in paradise. Moreover, it is said there is to be a multitude that no man can number in heaven; I have never read that there is to be a multitude that no man can number in hell. But I rejoice to know that the souls of all infants, as soon as they die, speed their way to paradise. Think what a multitude there is of them! And then there are the just, and the redeemed of all nations and kindreds up till now; and there are better times coming, when the religion of Christ shall be universal; when he shall reign from pole to pole with illimitable sway; when kingdoms shall bow before him, and nations be born in a day; and in the thousand years of the great millennial state there will be enough saved to make up all the deficiencies of the thousands of years that have gone before. Christ shall have the pre-eminence at last; his train shall be far larger than that which shall attend the chariots of the grim monarch of hell. Christ shall be master everywhere, and his praise sounded in every land. One hundred and forty-four thousand were observed, the types and representatives of a far larger number who are ultimately to be saved.

But notice, whilst the number is very large, *how very certain it is*. By turning over the leaves of your Bible to a previous chapter of this book, you will see that at the 4th verse it is written, that one hundred and forty-four thousand were sealed; and now we find there are one hundred and forty-four thousand saved; not 143,999, and 144,001, but exactly the number that are sealed. Now, my friends may not like what I am going to say; but if they do not like it, their quarrel is with God's Bible, not with me. There will be just as many in heaven as are sealed by God—just as many as Christ did purchase with his blood; all of them, and no more and no less. There will be just as many there as were quickened to life by the Holy Spirit, and were, "born again, not of blood, nor of the will of the flesh, nor of the will of man, but of God." "Ah," some say, "there is that abominable doctrine of election." Exactly so, if it be abominable; but you will never be able to cut it out of the Bible. You may hate it, and gnash and grind your teeth against it; but, remember, we can trace the pedigree of this doctrine, even apart from Scripture, to the time of the apostles. Church of England ministers and members, you have no right to differ from me on the doctrine of election, if you are what you profess by your own Articles. You who love the old

Puritans, you have no right to quarrel with me; for where will you find a Puritan who was not a strong Calvinist? You who love the fathers, you cannot differ from me. What say you of Augustine? Was he not, in his day, called a great and mighty teacher of grace? And I even turn to Roman Catholics, and, with all the errors of their system, I remind them that even in their body have been found those who have held that doctrine, and, though long persecuted for it, have never been expelled the church. I refer to the Jansenists. But, above all, I challenge every man who reads his Bible to say that that doctrine is not there. What saith the 9th of Romans? "The children being not yet born, neither having done any good or evil, that the purpose of God according to election might stand, not of works, but of him that calleth: It was said unto her, The elder shall serve the younger." And then it goes on to say to the carping objector—"Nay, but, O man, who art thou that repliest against God? Shall the thing formed say to him that formed it, Why hast thou made me thus? Hath not the potter power over the clay, of the same lump to make one vessel unto honour, and another unto dishonor?" But enough on this subject.

One hundred and forty-four thousand, we say, is a certain number made to represent the certainty of the salvation of all God's elect, believing people. Now, some say that this doctrine has a tendency to discourage men from coming to Christ. Well, you say so; but I have never seen it, and blessed be God I have never proved it so. I have preached this doctrine ever since I began to preach; but I can say this,—ye shall not (and I am now become a fool in glorying) ye shall not find among those who have not preached the doctrine, one who has been the instrument of turning more harlots, more drunkards, and more sinners of every class, from the error of their ways, than I have, by the simple preaching of the doctrine of free grace; and, while this has been so, I hold that no argument can be brought to prove that it has a tendency to discourage sinners, or bolster them up in sin. We hold, as the Bible says, that all the elect, and those only, shall be saved; all who go to Christ are elect. So that if any of you have in your heart a desire after heaven and after Christ; if you carry out that desire in sincere and earnest prayer, and are born again, you may as certainly conclude your election as you can conclude that you are alive. You must have been chosen of God before the foundation of the world, or you would never have done any of these things, seeing they are the fruits of election.

But why should it keep any one from going to Christ? "Because," says one, "if I go to Christ I may not be elect." No, sir, if you go, you prove that you are elect. "But," says another, "I am afraid to go, in case I should not be elect." Say as an old woman once said, "If there were only three persons elected, I would try to be one of them; and since he said, 'He that believeth shall be saved,' I would challenge God on his promise, and try if he would break it." No, come to Christ; and if you do so, beyond a doubt you are God's elect from the foundation of the world; and therefore this grace has been given to you. But why should it discourage you? Suppose there are a number of sick folk here, and a large hospital has been built. There is put up over the door, "All persons who come shall be taken in:" at the same time it is known that there is a person inside the hospital, who is so wise that he knows all who will come, and has written down the names of all who will come in a book, so that, when they come, those who open the doors will only say, "How marvellously wise our Master was, to know the names of those who would come." Is there anything despiriting in that? You would go, and you would have all the more confidence in that man's wisdom, because he was able to know before that they were going. "Ah, but," you say, "it was ordained that some should come." Well, to give you another illustration; suppose there is a rule that there always must be a thousand persons, or a very large number in the hospital. You say, "When I go perhaps they will take me in, and perhaps they will not." "But," says someone, "there is a rule that there must be a thousand in: somehow or other they must make up that number of beds, and have that number of patients in the hospital." You say, 'Then why should not I be among the thousand; and have not I the encouragement that whosoever goes shall not be cast out? And have I not again the encouragement, that if they will not go, they must be fetched in somehow or other; for the number must be made up; so it is determined and so it is decreed." You would therefore have a double encouragement, instead of half a one; and you would go with confidence, and say, "They must take me in, because they say they will take all in that come; and on the other hand, they must take me in, because they must have a certain number: that number is not made up, and why should not I be one?" Oh, never doubt about election; believe in Christ, and then rejoice in election; do not fret about it till you have believed in Christ.

"I looked, and, lo, a Lamb stood on the Mount Sion, and with him an hundred forty and four thousand." And who were these people, "having his Father's name written in their foreheads?" Not *B*s for "Baptists," not *W*s for "Wesleyans," not *E*s for "Established Church:" they had their Father's name and nobody else's. What a deal of fuss is made on earth about our distinctions! We think such a deal about belonging to this denomination, and the other. Why, if you were to go to heaven's gates, and ask if they had any Baptists there, the angel would only look at you, and not answer you; if you were to ask if they had any Wesleyans, or members of the Established Church, he would say, "Nothing of the sort;" but if you were to ask him whether they had any Christians there, "Ay," he would say, "an abundance of them: they are all one now—all called by one name; the old brand has been obliterated, and now they have not the name of this man or the other; they have the name of God, even their Father, stamped on their brow." Learn then dear friends, whatever the connection to which you belong, to be charitable to your brethren, and kind to them, seeing that, after all, the name you now hold here will be forgotten in heaven, and only your Father's name will be there known.

One more remark here, and we will turn from the worshippers to listen to their song. It is said of all these worshippers that they learned the song before they went there. At the end of the third verse it is said, "No man could learn that song but the hundred and forty and four thousand, which were redeemed from the earth." Brethren, we must begin heaven's song here below, or else we shall never sing it above. The choristers of heaven have all had rehearsals upon earth, before they sing in that orchestra. You think that, die when you may, you will go to heaven, without being prepared. Nay, sir; heaven is a prepared place for a prepared people, and unless you are "made meet to be partakers of the inheritance of the saints in light," you can never stand there among them. If you were in heaven without a new heart and a right spirit, you would be glad enough to get out of it; for heaven, unless a man is heavenly himself, would be worse than hell. A man who is unrenewed and unregenerate going to heaven would be miserable there. There would be a song—he could not join in it; there would be a constant hallelujah, but he would not know a note: and besides, he would be in the presence of the Almighty, even in the presence of the God he hates, and how could he be happy there? No, sirs; ye must learn the song of paradise here, or else ye can never sing it. Ye must learn to sing—

"Jesus, I love thy charming name,
'Tis music to my ears."

You must learn to feel that "sweeter sounds than music knows mingle in your Saviour's name," or else you can never chaunt the hallelujahs of the blest before the throne of the great "I AM." Take that thought, whatever else you forget; treasure it up in your memory, and ask grace of God that you may here be taught to sing the heavenly song, that afterwards in the land of the hereafter, in the home of the beautified, you may continually chaunt the high praises of him that loved you.

III. And now we come to the third and most interesting point, namely, THE LISTENING TO THEIR SONG. "I heard a voice form heaven, as the voice of many waters, and as the voice of a great thunder: and I heard the voice of harpers harping with their harps;" singing—how loud and yet how sweet!

First, then, singing *how loud*! It is said to be "like the voice of many waters." Have you never heard the sea roar, and the fulness thereof? Have you never walked by the sea-side, when the waves were singing, and when every little pebble-stone did turn chorister, to make up music to the Lord God of hosts? And have you never in time of storm beheld the sea, with its hundred hands, clapping them in gladsome adoration of the Most High? Have you never heard the sea roar out his praise, when the winds were holding carnival—perhaps singing the dirge of mariners, wrecked far out on the stormy deep, but far more likely exalting God with their hoarse voice, and praising him who makes a thousand fleets sweep over them in safety, and writes his furrows on their own youthful brow? Have you never heard the rumbling and booming of ocean on the shore, when it has been lashed into fury and has been driven upon the cliffs? If you have, you have a faint idea of the melody of heaven. It was "as the voice of many waters." But do not suppose that it is the whole of the idea. It is not the voice of one ocean, but the voice of many, that is needed to give you an idea of the melodies of heaven. You are to suppose ocean piled upon ocean, sea upon sea,—the Pacific piled upon the Atlantic, the Arctic upon that, the Antarctic higher still, and so ocean upon ocean, all lashed to fury, and all sounding with a mighty voice the praise of God. Such is the singing of heaven. Or if the illustration, fails to strike, take another. We have mentioned here two or three times the mighty falls of Niagara. They can be heard at a tremendous distance, so awful is their sound. Now, suppose waterfalls dashing upon waterfalls, cataracts upon cataracts, Niagaras upon Niagaras, each of them sounding forth their mighty voices, and you have got some idea of the singing of paradise. "I heard a voice like the voice of many waters." Can you not hear it? Ah! if our ears were opened we might almost cast the song. I have thought sometimes that the voice of the Aeolian harp, when it has swollen out grandly, was almost like an echo of the songs of those who sing before the throne; and on the summer eve, when the wind has come in gentle zephyrs through the forest, you might almost think it was the floating of some stray notes that had lost their way among the harps of heaven, and come down to us, to give us some faint foretaste of that song which hymns out in mighty peals before the throne of the Most High. But why so loud? The answer is, because there are so many there to sing. Nothing is more grand than the singing of multitudes. Many have been the persons who have told me that they could but weep when they heard you sing in this assembly, so mighty seemed the sound when all the people sang—

"Praise God from whom all blessings flow."

And, indeed, there is something very grand in the singing of multitudes. I remember hearing 12,000 sing on one occasion in the open air. Some of our friends were then present, when we concluded our service with that glorious hallelujah. Have you ever forgotten it? It was indeed a mighty sound; it seemed to make heaven itself ring again. Think, then, what must be the voice of those who stand on the boundless plains of heaven, and with all their might shout, "Glory and honour and power and dominion unto him that sitteth on the throne, and to the Lamb for ever and ever."

On reason, however, why the song is so loud is a very simple one, namely, because all those who are there think themselves bound to sing the loudest of all. You know our favourite hymn—

"Then loudest of the crowd I'll sing,
While heav'n's resounding mansions ring
With shouts of sov'reign grace."

And every saint will join that sonnet, and each one lift up his heart to God, then how mighty must be the strain of praise that will rise up to the throne of the glorious God our Father!

But note next, while it was a loud voice, how *sweet* it was. Noise is not music. There may be "a voice like many waters." and yet no music. It was sweet as well as loud; for John says, "I heard the voice of harpers harping with their harps." Perhaps the sweetest of all instruments is the harp. There are others which give forth sounds more grand and noble, but the harp is the sweetest of all instruments. I have sometimes sat to hear a skilful harper, till I could say, "I could sit and hear myself away," whilst with skilful fingers he touched the chords gently, and brought forth strains of melody which flowed like liquid silver, or like sounding honey into one's soul. Sweet, sweet beyond sweetness; words can scarcely tell how sweet the melody. Such is the music of heaven. No jarring notes there, no discord, but all one glorious harmonious song. You will not be there, formalist, to spoil the tune; nor you, hypocrite, to mar the melody; there will be all those there whose hearts are right with God, and therefore the strain will be one great harmonious whole, without a discord. Truly do we sing—

> "No groans to mingle with the songs
> That warble from immortal tongues."

And there will be no discord of any other sort to spoil the melody of those before the throne. Oh! my beloved brethren, that we might be there! Lift us up, ye cherubs! Stretch your wings, and bear us up where the sonnets fill the air. But if ye must not, let us wait our time.

> "A few more rolling suns at most,
> Will land us on fair Canaan's coast;"

and then we shall help to make the song, which now we can scarcely conceive, but which yet we desire to join.

IV. We now close with a remark upon the last point: WHY IS THE SONG SAID TO BE A NEW SONG? But one remark here. It will be a new song, because the saints were never in such a position before as they will be when they sing this new song. They are in heaven now; but the scene of our text is something more than heaven. It refers to the time when all the chosen race shall meet around the throne, when the last battle shall have been fought, and the last warrior shall have gained his crown. It is not now that they are thus singing, but it is in the glorious time to come, when all the hundred and forty and four thousand—or rather, the number typified by that number— will be all safely housed and all secure. I can conceive the period. Time was— eternity now reigns. The voice of God exclaims, "Are my beloved all safe?" The angel flies through paradise and returns with this message, "Yea, they are." "Is *Fearful* safe? Is Feeble-mind safe? Is Ready-to-Halt safe? Is Despondency safe?" "Yes, O king, they are," says he. "Shut-to the gates," says the Almighty, "they have been open night and day; shut them to now." Then, when all of them shall be there, then will be the time when the shout shall be louder than many waters, and the song shall begin which will never end. There is a story told in the history of brave Oliver Cromwell, which I use here to illustrate this new song. Cromwell and his Ironsides before they went to battle bowed the knee in prayer, and asked for God's help. Then, with their Bibles in their breasts, and their swords in their hands—a strange and unjustifiable mixture, but which their ignorance must excuse—they cried, "The Lord of hosts is with us, the God of Jacob is our refuge;" and rushing to battle they sang—

"O Lord our God, arise and let
Thine enemies scattered be,
And let all those that do thee hate
Before thy presence flee.

They had to fight up hill for a long time, but at last the enemy fled. The Ironsides were about to pursue them and win the booty, when the stern harsh voice of Cromwell was heard—"Halt! halt! now the victory is won, before you rush to the spoil return thanks to God;" and they sang some such song as this—"Sing unto the Lord, for he has gotten us the victory! Sing unto the Lord." It was said to have been one of the most majestic sights in that strange, yet good man's history. (I say that word without blushing, for good he was.) For a time the hills seemed to leap, whilst the vast multitude, turning from the slain, still stained with blood, lifted up their hearts to God. We say, again, it was a strange sight, yet a glad one. But how great shall be that sight, when Christ shall be seen as a conqueror, and when all his warriors, fighting side by side with him, shall see the dragon beaten in pieces beneath their feet. Lo, their enemies are fled; they were driven like thin clouds before a Biscay gale. They are all gone, death is vanquished, Satan is cast into the lake of fire, and here stands the King himself, crowned with many crowns, the victor of the victors. And in the moment of exaltation the Redeemer will say, "Come let us sing unto the Lord;" and then, louder than the shout of many waters, they shall sing, "Hallelujah! the Lord God Omnipotent reigneth." Ah! that will be the full carrying out of the great scene! My feeble words cannot depict it. I send you away with this simple question, "Shall *you* be there to see the conqueror crowned?" Have *you* "a good hope through grace" that you shall? If so, be glad; if not, go to your houses, fall on your knees, and pray to God to save you from that terrible place which must certainly be your portion, instead of that great heaven of which I preach, unless you turn to God with full purpose of heart.

7

Heavenly Rest

"There remaineth therefore a rest to the people of God."

—Hebrews 4:9

THE APOSTLE PROVED, IN THE former part of this and the latter part of the preceding chapter, that there was a rest promised in Scripture called the rest of God. He proved that Israel did not attain that rest for God sware in his wrath, saying, "They shall not enter into my rest." He proved that this did not merely refer to the rest of the land of Canaan; for he says that after they were in Canaan, David himself speaks again in after ages concerning the rest of God, as a thing which was yet to come. Again he proves, that "seeing those to whom it was promised did not enter in, because of unbelief, and it remaineth that some must enter in, therefore," saith he, "there remaineth a rest to the people of God."

"*My* rest," says God: the rest of God! Something more wonderful than any other kind of rest. In my text it is (in the original) called the *Sabbatism*—not the Sabbath, but the rest of the Sabbath—not the outward ritual of the Sabbath, which was binding upon the Jew, but the inward spirit of the sabbath, which is the joy and delight of the Christian. "There remaineth therefore"—because others have not had it, because some are to have it—"There remaineth therefore a rest to the people of God."

Now, this rest, I believe, is partly enjoyed on earth. "We that have believed do enter into rest," for we have ceased from our own works, as God did from his. But the full fruition and rich enjoyment of it remains in the future and eternal state of the beatified on the other side the stream of death. Of that it shall be our delightful work to talk a little this morning. And oh! if God should help me to raise but one of his feeble saints on the wings of love to look within the veil, and see the joys of the future, I shall be well contented to have made the joy-bells ring in one heart at least, to have set one eye flashing with joy, and to have made one spirit light with gladness. The rest of heaven! I shall try first to *exhibit it* and then to *extol it.*

I. First, I shall try to EXHIBIT the rest of heaven; and in doing so I shall exhibit it, first by way of contrast, and then by way of comparison.

1. To begin then, I shall try to exhibit heaven *by way of contrast*. The rest of the righteous in glory is now to be contrasted with certain other things.

We will contrast it, first, *with the best estate of the worldling and the sinner.* The worldling has frequently a good estate. Sometimes his vats overflow, his barns are crammed, his heart is full of joy and gladness, there are periods with him when he flourishes like a green bay tree, when field is added to field, and house to house, when he pulls down his barns and builds greater, when the river of his joy is full, and the ocean of his life is at its flood with joy and blessedness. But sh! beloved, the state of the righteous up there is not for a moment to be compared with the joy of the sinner;—it is so infinitely superior, so far surpassing it, that it seems impossible that I should even try to set it in contrast. The worldling, when his corn and his wine are increased, has a glad eye and A joyous heart; but even then he has the direful thought that *he may soon leave his wealth.* He remembers that death may cut him down, that he must then leave all his fair riches behind him, and sleep like the meanest of the land in a narrow coffin, six feet of earth his only heritage. Not so the righteous man: he has obtained an inheritance which is "undefiled, and that fadeth not away." He knows that there is no possibility of his losing his joys;

"He is securely blessed,
Has done with sin, and care, and woe,
And doth with Jesus rest."

He has no dread of dissolution, no fear of the coffin or the shroud, and so far the life of heaven is not worthy to be put in comparison with the life of the sinner. But the worldling, with all his joys, always has *a worm at the root* of them. Ye votaries of pleasure! the blush upon your cheek is frequently but a painted deception. Ah! ye sons and daughters of gaiety! the light foot of your dance is not in keeping with the heavy woe of your miserable spirits. Do you not confess that if by the excitement of company you for awhile forget the emptiness of your heart, yet silence, and the hour of midnight, and the waking watches of your bed, bid you sometimes think that there must be something more blessed than the mere wanderings of gaiety in which you now are found? You are trying the world some of you; speak then! Do you not find it empty? Might it not be said of the world, as an old philosopher said of it when he represented a man with it in his hands smiting it and listening to its ringing? Touch it, touch it I make it ring again; it is empty. So it is with the world. You know it is so; and if you know it not as yet, the day is coming when after you have plucked the sweets you shall be pricked with the thorn, and when you shall find that all is unsatisfactory that does not begin and end with God. Not so the Christian in heaven. For him there are no nights; and if there be times of solitude and rest, he is ever filled with ecstatic joy. His river floweth ever full of bliss, without one pebble of sorrow over which it ripples, he has no aching conscience, no "aching void the world can never fill." He is supremely blessed, satisfied with favor, and full with the goodness of the Lord. And ye know, ye worldlings, that your best estates often bring you great anxiety, *lest they should depart from you.* You are not so foolish yet as to conceive that riches endure for ever. You men of business are frequently led to see that riches take to themselves wings and fly away. You have accumulated a fortune; but you find it is harder to retain than it is to get. You are seeking after a competence; but you find that you grasp at shadows that flit away—that the everlasting vicissitudes of business and the constant changes of mankind are causes of prudent alarm to you, for you fear that you shall lose your gods, and that your gourd shall be eaten by the worm, and fall down, and your shadow shall be taken away. Not so the Christian. He lives in a house that can never hasten to decay; he wears a crown, the glister of which shall never be dim; he has a garment which shall never wax old; he has bliss that never can depart from him, nor he from it. He is now firmly set, like a pillar of marble in the temple of God. The world may rock, the tempest may sway it like the cradle of a child; but there, above the world, above the perpetual revolution of the stars, the Christian stands secure and immovable; trio rest infinitely surpasseth yours. Ah I ye shall go to all the fabled luxuries of eastern monarchs, and see their dainty couches and their luscious wines. Behold the riches of their pleasantry! How charming is the music that lulls them to their sleep! How gently moves the fan that wafts them to their slumber! But ah!

> "I would not change my blest estate
> For all the world calls good or great;
> And whilst my faith can keep her hold
> I envy not the sinner's gold"—

I reckon that the richest, highest, noblest condition of a worldly man is not worthy to be compared with the joy-that is to be revealed hereafter in the breasts of those who are sanctified. O ye spendthrift mortals, that for one merry dance and a giddy life will lose a world of joys! O fools that catch at bubbles and lose realities! O ten thousand times mad men, that grasp at shadows and lose the substance! What! sirs do you think a little round of pleasure, a few years of gaiety and merriment, just a little time of the tossing about, to and fro, of worldly business, is a compensation for eternal ages of unfading bliss! Oh! how foolish will you conceive yourselves to be, when you are in the next state, when cast away from heaven you will see the saints blessed! I think I hear your mournful soliloquy, "Oh! how cheaply did I sell my soul! What a poor price did I get for all I have now lost! I have lost the palace and the crown, and the joy and bliss for ever, and am shut up in hell! And for what did I lose it? I lost it for the lascivious wanton kiss. I lost it for the merry drunken song; I lost it for just a few short years of pleasures, which, after all, were only painted pleasures!" Oh! I think I see you in your lost estates, cursing yourselves, rending your hair, that you should have sold heaven for counters and have changed away eternal life for pitiful farthings, which were spent quickly and which burned your hand in the spending of them! Oh! that ye were wise, that ye would weigh those things, and reckon that a life of the greatest happiness here is nothing compared with the glorious hereafter: "There remaineth a rest to the people of God."

Now let me put it in *more pleasing contrast.* I shall contrast the rest of the believer above with the miserable estate of the believer sometimes here below. Christians have their sorrows. Suns have their spots skies have their clouds, and Christians have their sorrows too. But oh! how different will the state of the righteous be up there, from the state of the believer here! Here the Christian has to suffer anxiety. He is anxious to serve his Master, to do his best in his day and generation His constant cry is—"Help me to serve thee, O my God," and he looks out, day after day, with a strong desire for opportunities of doing good. Ah! if he be an active Christian, he will have much labor, much toil, in endeavoring to serve his Master; and there will be times when he will say, "My soul is in haste to be gone; I am not wearied of the labor, I am wearied in it. To toil thus in the sun, though for a good Master, is not the thing that just now I desire." Ah! Christian, the day shall soon be over, and thou shalt no longer have to toil; the sun is nearing the horizon; it shall rise again with a brighter day than thou hast ever seen before. There, up in heaven, Luther has no more to face a thundering Vatican; Paul has no more to run from city to city, and continent to continent, there Baxter has no more to toil in his pulpit, to preach with a broken heart to hard hearted sinners, there no longer has Knox to "cry aloud and spare not" against the immoralities of the false church; there no more shall be the strained lung, and the tired throat, and the aching eye; no more shall the sunday school teacher feel that his sabbath is a day of joyful weariness; no more shall the tract distributor meet with rebuffs. No, there, those who have served their country and their God, those who have toiled for man's welfare, with all their might, shall enter into everlasting rest. Sheathed is the sword, the banner is furled, the fight is over, the victory won; and they rest from their labors.

Here, too, the Christian is always *sailing onward*, he is always in motion he feels that he has not yet attained. Like Paul he can say "Forgetting the things that are behind, I press forward to that which is before." But there his weary head shall be crowned with unfading light. There the ship that has been speeding onward shall furl its sails in the port of eternal bliss. There he who, like an arrow, has sped his way shall be fixed for ever in the target. There we who like fleeting clouds were driven by every wind, shall gently distil in one perennial shower of everlasting joy. There is no progress, no motion there; they are at rest, they have attained the summit of the mountain, they have ascended to their God and our God. Higher they cannot go; they have reached the *Ultima Thule*, there are no fortunate islands beyond; this is life's utmost end of happiness; and they furl their sails, rest from their labors, and enjoy themselves for aye. There is a difference between the progress of earth and the perfect fixity of the rest of hearer.

Here, too, the believer is often the subject of *doubt and fear*. "Am I his or am I not?" is often the cry. He trembleth lest he should be deceived, at times he almost despairs, and is inclined not to put his name down as one of the children of God. Dark insinuations are whispered into his ears, he thinks that God's mercy is clean gone for ever, and that he will not be mindful of him any more. Again, his sins some times upbraid him, and he thinks God will not have mercy on him. He has a poor fainting heart; he is like Ready-to-halt, he has to go all his way on crutches; he has a poor feeble mind, always tumbling down over a straw, and fearing one day he shall be drowned in a cart-rut. Though the lions are chained he is as much afraid of them as if they were loose. Hill Difficulty often afrights him; going down into the valley of humiliation is often troublesome work to him; but there, there are no hills to climb, no dragons to fight, no foes to conquer, no dangers to dread. Ready-to-halt, when he dies, will bury his crutches, and Feeblemind will leave his feebleness behind him; Fearing will never fear again; poor Doubting-heart will learn confidently to believe. Oh, joy above all joys! The day is coming when I shall "know as I am known," when I shall not want to ask whether I am his or not, for in his arms encircled, there shall be no room for doubt. Oh! Christian, you think there are slips between your lips and that cup of joy, but when you grasp the handle of that cup with your hand, and are drinking draughts of ineffable delight, then you will have no doubt or fear.

"There you shall see his face,
And never, never sin
There from the rivers of his grace,
Drink endless pleasures in."

Here, too, on earth, the Christian has to *suffer;* here he has the aching head and the pained body; his limbs may be bruised or broken, disease may rack him with torture; he may be an afflicted one from his birth, he may have lost an eye or an ear or he may have lost many of his powers; or if not, being of a weakly constitution he may have to spend the most of his days and nights upon the bed of weariness. Or if his body be sound, yet what suffering he has in his mind! Conflicts between depravity and gross temptations from the evil one, assaults of hell, perpetual attacks of divers kinds, from the world, the flesh, and the devil. But there, no aching head no weary heart; there no palsied arm, no brow ploughed with the furrows of old age; there the lost limb shall be recovered, and old age shall find itself endowed with perpetual youth, there the infirmities of the flesh shall be left behind, given to the worm and devoured by corruption. There they shall flit, as on the wings of angels, from pole to pole, and from place to place, without weariness or anguish; there they shall never need to lie upon the bed of rest, or the bed of suffering, for day without night, with joy unflagging, they shall circle God's throne rejoicing, and ever praise him who hath said, "The inhabitants there shall never be sick."

There, too, they shall be free from *persecution.* Here Sicilian Vespers, and St. Bartholomew, and Smithfield, are well-known words; but there shall be none to taunt them with a cruel word, or touch them with a cruel hand. There emperors and kings are not known, and those who had power to torture them cease to be. They are in the society of saints; they shall be free from all the idle converse of the wicked, and from their cruel jeers set free for ever. Set free from persecution! Ye army of martyrs, ye were slain, ye were torn asunder, ye were cast to wild beasts, ye wandered about in sheep skins and goats' skins, destitute, afflicted, and tormented. I see you now, a mighty host. The habiliments you wear are torn with thorns; your faces are scarred with sufferings; I see you at your stakes, and on your crosses; I hear your words of submission on your racks, I see you in your prisons, I behold you in your pillories—but,

"Now ye are arrayed in white,
Brighter than the noonday-sun

94

Fairest of the sons of light,
Nearest the eternal throne."

These are they, who "for their Master died, who love the cross and crown;" they waded through seas of blood, in order to obtain the inheritance; and there they are, with the blood-red crown of martyrdom about their heads, that ruby brightness, far excelling every other. Yes, there is no persecution there. "There remaineth a rest for the people of God."

Alas! in this mortal state the child of God is also subject to *sin;* even he faileth in his duty, and wandereth from his God; even he doth not walk in all the law of his God blameless, though he desireth to do it. Sin now troubleth him constantly; but there sin is dead, there they have no temptation to sin, from without or from within, but they are perfectly free to serve their Master. Here the child of God has sometimes to weep repentingly of his backslidings; but there they never shed tears of penitence, for they have never cause to do so.

And last of all, here, the child of God has to wet the cold ashes of his relatives with *tears;* here he has to bid adieu to all that is lovely and fair of mortal race; here it is he hears, "earth to earth, and dust to dust, and ashes to ashes," while the solemn music of the dust upon the coffin lid beats doleful time to those words. Here is the mother buried, the child snatched away, the husband rent from the bosom of a loving wife, the brother parted from the sister. The plate upon the coffin, the last coat of arms of earth, earth's last emblems are here ever before our eyes. But there never once shall be heard the toll of the funeral bell, no hearse with plumes has ever darkened the streets of gold, no emblems of sorrow have ever intruded into the homes of the immortal, they are strangers to the meaning of death; they cannot die— they live for ever, having no power to decay, and no possibility of corruption. Oh! rest of the righteous, how blest art thou, where families shall again be bound up in one bundle, where parted friends shall again meet to part no more, and where the whole church of Christ united in one mighty circle, shall together praise God and the Lamb throughout eternal ages.

Brethren, I have tried thus to set the rest of the righteous in the way of contrast; I feel I have failed. Poor are the words I can utter to tell you of immortal things Even holy Baxter himself, when he wrote of the "Saints' Rest," paused and said; "But these are only tinklings compared with the full thunders of heaven." I cannot tell you, dear friends, nor can mortal tell, what God hath prepared for them that love him.

2. And now I shall try very briefly to exhibit this contrast *in the way of comparison*. The Christian hath some rest here, but nothing compared with the rest which is to come.

There is the *rest of the church*. When the believer joins the church of God, and becomes united with them, he may expect to rest. The good old writer of the "Pilgrim's Progress," says, that when the weary pilgrims were once admitted to the house Beautiful, they were shown to sleep in a chamber called peace," or "rest." The church-member at the Lord's table has a sweet enjoyment of rest in fellowship with the saints; but ah! up there the rest of church fellowship far surpasses anything that is known here; for there are no divisions there, no angry words at the church meetings, no harsh thoughts of one another, no bickerings about doctrine, no fightings about practice. There Baptist, and Presbyterian, and Independent, and Wesleyan, and Episcopalian, serving the same Lord, and having been washed in the same blood, sing the same song, and are all joined in one. There pastors and deacons never look coolly on each other; no haughty prelates here, no lofty-minded ministers there, but all meek and lowly, all knit together in brotherhood; they have a rest which surpasseth all the rest of the church on earth.

There is, again, a rest of *faith* which a Christian enjoys; a sweet rest. Many of us have known it. We have known what it is, when the billows of trouble have run high, to hide ourselves in the breast of Christ, and feel secure. We have cast our anchor deep into the rocks of God's promise, we have gone to sleep in our chamber and have not feared the tempest, we have looked at tribulation, and have smiled at, we have looked at death himself, and have laughed him to scorn, we have had much trust by Christian faith that, dauntless and fearless, nothing could move us. Yes, in the midst of calumny, reproach, slander and contempt, we have said, "I shall not be moved, for God is on my side." But the rest up there is better still more unruffled, more sweet, more perfectly calm, more enduring, and more lasting than even the rest of faith.

And, again, the Christian sometimes has the blessed rest of *communion*. There are happy moments when he puts his head on the Saviour's breast—when, like John, he feels that he is close to the Saviour's heart, and there he sleeps. "God giveth his beloved sleep;" not the sleep of unconsciousness, but the sleep of joy. Happy, happy, happy are the dreams we have had on the couch of communion; blessed have been the times, when, like the spouse in Solomon's song, we could say of Christ, "His left hand was under my head, and with his right hand did he embrace me."

96

"But sweeter still the fountain head,
Though sweet may be the stream;"

When we shall have plunged into a very bath of joy, we shall have found the delights even of communion on earth to have been but the dipping of the finger in the cup, but the dipping of the bread in the dish, whereas heaven itself shall be the participation of the whole of the joy, and not the mere antepast of it. Here we sometimes enter into the portico of happiness, there we shall go into the presence chamber of the King, here we look over the hedge and see the flowers in heaven's garden, there we shall walk between the beds of bliss, and pluck fresh flowers at each step; here we just look and see the sunlight of heaven in the distance, like the lamps of the thousand-gated cities shining afar off, but there we shall see them in all their blaze of splendor, here we listen to the whisperings of heaven's melody, borne by winds from afar; but there, entranced, amidst the grand oratorio of the blessed, we shall join in the everlasting hallelujah to the great Messiah, the God, the I AM. Oh! again I say, do we not wish to mount aloft, and fly away, to enter into the rest which remaineth to the people of God?

II. And now, yet more briefly, and then we shall have done. I am to endeavor to EXTOL this rest, as I have tried to EXHIBIT it. I would extol this rest for many reasons; and oh! that I were eloquent, that I might extol it as it deserves! Oh! for the lip of angel, and the burning tongue of cherub, to talk now of the bliss of the sanctified and of the rest of God's people!

It is, first, a *perfect* rest. They are wholly at rest in heaven. Here rest is but partial. I hope in a little time to cease from every-day labors for a season, but then the head will think, and the mind may be looking forward to prospective labor, and whilst the body is still, the brain will yet be in motion. Here, on Sabbath days a vast multitude of you sit in God's house, but many of you are obliged to stand, and rest but little except in your mind, and even when the mind is at rest the body is wearied with the toil of standing. You have a weary mile perhaps, many miles, to go to your homes on the Sabbath day. And let the Sabbatarian say what he will, you may work on the Sabbath day, if you work for God; and this Sabbath day's work of going to the house of God is work for God, and God accepts it. For yourselves you may not labor, God commands you to rest, but if you have to toil these three, these four, these five, these six miles, as many of you have done, I will not and I must not blame you. "The priests in the sanctuary profane the Sabbath, and are blameless." It is toil and labor, it is true but it is for a good cause—for your Master. But there, my friends, the rest is perfect; the body there rests perpetually, the mind too always rests; though the inhabitants are always busy, always serving God, yet they are never weary, never toil-worn, never fagged; they never fling themselves upon their couches at the end of the day, and cry, "Oh! when shall I be away from this land of oil?" They I never stand up in the burning sunlight, and wipe the hot sweat from their brow; they never rise from their bed in the morning, half refreshed, to go to laborious study. No, they are perfectly at rest, stretched on the couch of eternal joy. They know not the semblance of a tear; they have done with sin, and care, and woe, and, with their Saviour rest.

Again, it is a *seasonable* rest. How seasonable it will be for some of you! Ye sons of wealth, ye know not the toils of the poor; the horny-handed laborer, perhaps, you have not seen, and you not how he has to tug and to toil. Among my congregation I have many of a class, upon whom I have always looked with pity, poor women who must rise to-morrow morning with the sun, and begin that everlasting "stitch, stitch," that works their finger to the bone. And from Monday morning till Saturday night, many of you, my members, and multitudes of you, my hearers, will not be able to lay aside your needle and your thread, except when, tired and weary, you fall back on your chair, and are lulled to sleep by your thoughts of labor! Oh! how seasonable will heaven's rest be to you! Oh! how glad will you be, when you get there, to find that there are no Monday mornings, no more toil for you, but rest, eternal rest! Others of you have hard manual labor to perform; you have reason to thank God that you are strong enough to do it and you are not ashamed of your work; for labor is an honor to a man. But still there are times when you say, "I wish I were not so dragged to death by the business of London life." We have but little rest in this huge city, our day is longer, and our work is harder than our friends in the country. You have sometimes sighed to go into the green fields for a breath of fresh air, you have longed to hear the song of the sweet birds that used to wake you when you were lads; you have regretted the bright blue sky, the beauteous flowers, and the thousand charms of a country life. And perhaps, you will never get beyond this smoky city, but remember, when you get up there, "sweet fields arrayed in living green" and "rivers of delight" shall be the place where you shall rest, you shall have all the joys you can conceive of in that home of happiness; and though worn and weary, you come to your grave, tottering on your staff; having journeyed through the wilderness of life, like a weary camel, which has only stopped on the Sabbath to sip its little water at the well, or to be baited at the oasis, there you will arrive at your journey's end, laden with gold and spices, and enter into the grand caravanserai of heaven, and enjoy for ever the things you have wearily carried with you here.

And I must say, that to others of us who have not to toil with our hands, heaven will be a seasonable rest. Those of us who have to tire our brain day after day will find it no slight boon to have an everlasting rest above. I will not boast of what I may do, there may be many who do more, there may be many who are perpetually and daily striving to serve God, and are using their mind's best energies in so doing. But this much I may say, that almost every week I have the pleasure of preaching twelve times, and often in my sleep do I think of what I shall say next time. Not having the advantage of laying out my seven shillings and sixpence in buying manuscripts, it costs me hard diligent labor to find even something to say. And I sometimes have a difficulty to keep the hopper full in the mill, I feel that if I had not now and then a rest I should have no wheat for God's children. Still it is on, on, on, and on we must go, we hear the chariot wheels of God behind us, and we dare not stop, we think that eternity is drawing nigh, and we must go on. Rest to us now is more than labor, we want to be at work; but oh! how seasonable it shall be, when to the minister it shall be said—

"Servant of God, well done!
Rest from thy loved employ;
The battle fought, the victory won,
Enter thy Master's joy."

It will be seasonable rest. You that are weary with state cares, and have to learn the ingratitude of men; you that have sought honors, and have got them to your cost, you seek to do your best, but your very independence of spirit is called servility, whilst your servility would have been praised! You who seek to honor God, and not to honor men, who will not bind yourselves to parties, but seek in your own independent and honest judgment to serve your country and your God you, I say, when God shall see fit to call you to himself, will find it no small joy to have done with parliaments, to have done with states and kingdoms, and to have laid aside your honors, to receive honors more lasting amongst those who dwell for ever before the throne of the Most High.

One thing, and then once more, and then farewell. This rest, my brethren, ought to be extolled, because it is *eternal.* Here my best joys bear "mortar" on their brow; here my fair flowers fade; here my sweet cups have dregs and are soon empty; here my sweetest birds must die, and their melody must soon be hushed; here my most pleasant days must have their nights; here the flowings of my bliss must have their ebbs, everything doth pass away, but there everything shall be immortal; the harp shall be unrusted, the crown unwithered, the eye undimmed the voice unfaltering, the heart unwavering, and the being wholly consolidated unto eternity. Happy day, happy day, when mortality shall be swallowed up of life, and the mortal shall have put on immortality!

And then, lastly, this glorious rest is to be best of all commended for its *certainty*. "There remaineth a rest to the people of God." Doubting one, thou hast often said, "I fear I shall never enter heaven." Fear not, all the people of God shall enter there; there is no fear about it. I love the quaint saying of a dying man, who, in his country brogue, exclaimed, "I have no fear of going home; I have sent all before me. God's finger is on the latch of my door and I am ready for him to enter." "But," said one "are you not afraid least you should miss your inheritance?" "Nay," said he "nay, there is one crown in heaven that the angel Gabriel could not wear; it will fit no head but mine. There is one throne in heaven that Paul the apostle could not fill; it was made for me, and I shall have it. There is one dish at the banquet that I must eat, or else it will be untasted, for God has set it apart for me." O Christian, what a joyous thought! thy portion is secure! "there remaineth a rest." "But cannot I forfeit it?" No, it is entailed. If I be a child of God I shall not lose it. It is mine as securely as if I were there.

> "Come, Christian, mount to Pisgah's top,
> And view the landscape o'er."

Seest thou that little river of death, glistening in the sunlight, and across it dost thou see the pinnacles of the eternal city? Dost thou mark the pleasant suburbs and all the joyous inhabitants? Turn thine eye to that spot. Dost thou see where that ray of light is glancing now? There is a little spot there; dost thou see it? That is thy patrimony; that is thine. Oh, if thou couldst fly across thou wouldst see written upon it, "this remaineth for such an one, preserved for him only. He shall be caught up and dwell for ever with God." Poor doubting one; see thine inheritance; it is thine. If thou believest in the Lord Jesus thou art one of the Lord's people; if thou hast repented of sin thou art one of the Lord's people; if thou hast been renewed in heart thou art one of the Lord's people, and there is a place for thee, a crown for thee, a harp for thee. No one else shall have it but thyself, and thou shalt have it ere long. Just pardon me one moment if I beg of you to conceive of yourselves as being in heaven. Is it not a strange thing to think of—a poor clown in heaven? Think, how will you feel with your crown on your head? Weary matron, many years have rolled over you. How changed will be the scene when you are young again. Ah, toil-worn laborer, only think when thou shalt rest for aye. Canst thou conceive it? Couldst thou but think for a moment, of thyself as being in heaven now, what a strange surprise would seize thee. Thou wouldst not so as much say, "What! are these streets of gold? What! are these walls of jasper?" "What, am I here? in white? Am I here, with a crown on my brow? Am I here singing, that was always groaning? What! I praise God that once cursed him? What! I lifting up my voice in his honor? Oh, precious blood that washed me clean! Oh, precious faith that set me free! Oh, precious Spirit that made me repent, else I had been cast away and been in hell! But oh! what wonders! Angels! I am surprised. I am enraptured! Wonder of wonders! Oh! gates of pearls, I long since heard of you! Oh! joys that never fade, I long since heard tell of you! But I am like the Queen of Sheba, the half has not yet been told me. Profusion, oh profusion of bliss!— wonder of wonders!—miracle of miracles! What a world I am in! And oh! that I am here, this is the topmost miracle of all!" And yet 'tis true, 'tis true; and that is the glory of it. It is true. Come, worm, and prove it, come, pall; come shroud; come, and prove it. Then come wings of faith, come, leap like a seraph; come, eternal ages, come, and ye shall prove that there are joys that the eye hath not seen, which the ear hath not heard, and which only God can reveal to us by his spirit. Oh! my earnest prayer is, that none of you may come short of this rest, but that ye may enter into it, and enjoy it for ever and ever. God give you his great blessing, for Jesus sake! Amen.

Printed in Great Britain
by Amazon